D1634335

Other titles by the same authors:

The Walking Diet
Fitness Walking

Walk Slim

THE EASY WAY TO LOSE A STONE IN 30 DAYS

Les Snowdon and Maggie Humphreys

AUTHORS OF THE WORLDWIDE BESTSELLER
The Walking Diet

MAINSTREAM
PUBLISHING

EDINBURGH AND LONDON

First published in Great Britain in 1994 by
MAINSTREAM PUBLISHING COMPANY
(EDINBURGH) LTD
7 Albany Street
Edinburgh EH1 3UG

Reprinted 1994

ISBN 1 85158 604 0

A catalogue record for this book is available from the British
Library

Phototypeset in Janson 11/12pt by Intype, London

Printed and bound in Great Britain by
Biddles Ltd, Guildford and King's Lynn

If you are unfit, pregnant, or have a diagnosed medical problem
which will affect your ability to exercise, you should check with
your doctor before commencing a vigorous fitness walking
programme. The authors and publishers cannot accept
responsibility for any injury or damage suffered as a result of
attempting an exercise in this book.

To
Tim
with love

CONTENTS

ACKNOWLEDGMENTS

The authors gratefully acknowledge the following contributions in the preparation of this book: illustrations by Irene Barry; exercise illustrations devised by Sandra Sheffield, Fitness and Exercise Cert., SKFA; data/information from *The Composition of Foods and Supplements* reproduced with the permission of the Royal Society of Chemistry and the Controller of HMSO.

INTRODUCTION
Walking Works Wonders

Life is a maze
in which we take the wrong turning
before we have learned to walk
CYRIL CONNOLLY

If you want to lose weight, tone up your body and get slim;
if you want to watch the pounds drop away and have more
energy and vitality than you have ever had before; if you
want a simple way to get fit and stay fit for the rest of your
life – then *Walk Slim* is for you.

Easier than jogging, swimming or dance aerobics, man-
kind's simplest way of getting around is quickly becoming the
easiest and most effective way for most people to lose weight
and get fit. Almost a 'forgotten art', walking is fast becoming
the exercise of the 90s – and just about anyone can do it,
young and old.

During the past ten years walking has been at the forefront
of a fitness revolution that has swept America. It has become
known as 'the quiet revolution'. Walking for fitness or 'fitness
walking' has now replaced jogging and is the most widely
practised aerobic exercise used by more than 70 million
Americans to get fit, stay slim and beat stress.

Suddenly, fitness walking is the most popular and fashion-
able exercise to be seen doing. Cher, Arnold Schwarzenegger
and even 'go for the burn queen' Jane Fonda are all fitness
walkers.

Experts are now beginning to caution against the effects
that jogging has on the body. 'You can't use running as a lifetime exercise. The body was not built for running,' says Gary
Yanker, a walking expert. Biomechanical studies show that

your feet pound the ground with 3–4 times your body weight when jogging compared with only 1–1.5 times your body weight when you walk. This makes walking a safe and almost injury-free aerobic exercise for people of all ages.

According to the World Health Organisation, 'A walker loses weight, lowers cholesterol, reduces conditions associated with hypertension, slows ageing and the decline of aerobic capacity, increases strength, flexibility and balance, strengthens bones and increases stamina.'

The founding father of the medical profession, Hippocrates, said that walking is the best medicine. Now, 2500 years later, fitness walking is a 'best exercise' recommended in more than 40 medical studies by exercise physiologists, biomechanical experts, cardiologists, chest experts, obesity experts and stress experts.

The message is simple: fitness walking – brisk aerobic walking – is the easiest, cheapest and most accessible way for most people to get fit and stay fit for life. There is nothing difficult or faddish about walking, so it appeals to people of all ages. It keeps you slim, it helps beat stress – and it's fun.

You may have tried other fitness and weight loss routines and failed, but this time you are going to succeed. This time you're going to watch the pounds fall away forever. This time you are going to be a winner.

Tired of diet and exercise fads that don't work? Well, say goodbye to failure and hello to sweet, glorious success. *The Walk Slim Diet* plan will shift those unwanted pounds, tone and trim you. It will give you more energy and vitality than you've ever had. It's easy and it works. No matter how much weight you want to lose, walking and *The Walk Slim Diet* will work for you.

Because walking works wonders.

Fitness – It's Got to be Fun

We must walk before we run
GEORGE BORROW

In June 1992 the National Fitness Survey was published by the British Health Education Authority. The survey was carried out to assist the UK Government in developing policies and targets for increasing the activity and fitness of the population and to increase individual awareness of the benefits of 'active living'. The survey confirmed that the British are getting fatter, lazier and unhealthier:

- 48 per cent of men and 40 per cent of women are overweight
- nearly one third of men and two thirds of women find it difficult to walk at 3 mph up a gentle 1 in 20 slope without suffering breathlessness and fatigue
- for many women aged between 55 and 64, walking on level ground for longer than a few minutes is strenuous
- three in four people risk dying early through circulatory diseases related to lack of exercise
- some 70-year-old men are fitter than their 17-year-old granddaughters

The British are spending more time in their armchairs than exercising (other surveys show that some people are spending as much as 25 hours a week watching TV). Although 80 per cent of British people express a strong belief in the value of exercise, only a minority do anything about it.

'Modern living has taken much of the energy out of our lives and we need to find ways of putting it back,' said Dr Jacky Chambers, director of public health at the Health Education Authority.

And one of the *key messages* of the survey was for people to *'take longer walks more often and more briskly'*.

Several studies worldwide show that the least active among us are twice as likely to have a heart attack as the most active.

In the USA, a sedentary lifestyle is now considered so bad for you that the American Heart Association now lists it as a major 'risk factor' on a par with high blood cholesterol, high blood pressure and cigarette smoking. And *the exercise most recommended* to get fit, lose weight and reduce the factors that contribute to heart disease is **brisk walking**.

If exercise is so important in controlling our weight and in maintaining fitness and health, why is it so few people succeed in keeping it up? After all, the Fitness Survey found that 80 per cent of people expressed a strong belief in the value of exercise to health and fitness.

Before we answer that, we would like to remind you of a well-known story. Do you remember those wonderful children's classics, *Alice in Wonderland* and *Through the Looking Glass*? Do you remember the bit when the Red Queen seized Alice by the hand and dragged her faster and faster through the countryside, but no matter how fast they ran, they always stayed in the same place, and Alice saying: 'It takes all the running you can do to keep in the same place'?

A familiar story – yes?

For many of us, exercise is a bit like this. No matter how much we exercise we never seem to make any progress. It's the yo-yo fitness syndrome: you yo-yo up and down between one exercise routine and another trying to find one that works for you and that you can keep up.

Unfortunately, the statistics speak for themselves: 25 per cent of people starting out on fitness programmes today will give them up within a week; 60 per cent of those starting out on jogging programmes today will drop out or burn out within three months. Yet many of those same people will be back at it within a few months and they will be trying exercise bikes, aerobics, swimming, rowing, skipping and so on. Like yo-yo dieters, they will yo-yo up and down from one activity to another, and each time they will fail.

Why? Because they're not having any fun.

Five years ago we weren't having any fun! When it came to exercise that is.

Walking Off Weight

It's because exercise and dieting is so little fun that more than 90 per cent of people starting out on diet and fitness routines fail. If it's not fun, you won't keep it up.

Five years ago we were overweight and unfit and we were tired of trying every exercise and diet routine under the sun – jogging, cycling, swimming, squash, skipping, exercise bikes and a dozen other exercise and diet routines available in print and video. We were part of the 90 per cent of people who continually fail. We were tired, bored and we had made little progress in losing weight and getting fit.

Until we discovered *fitness walking*.

We had always loved walking, but we had tended to walk at weekends when we had more time. Discovering fitness walking was like finding the Holy Grail of fitness. Instead of waiting for the weekend, we decided to get out and walk four or five times a week, starting at our own front door and doing a circuit around the block and back. And we set out to walk at a brisker pace, stepping up our speed to 4 mph.

Within a month we were regularly doing 30-minute walks and we had more energy to get through the day. We felt fitter and more alert and with the low-fat, high-fibre diet we had begun, the pounds were beginning to drop off.

The rest, as they say, is history.

We put our fitness walking experiences down on paper and they became a popular bestseller *The Walking Diet*. The book was published in Britain in April 1991 and has since been published in eight countries around the world including Australia and the USA.

Everywhere we have travelled over the past few years, people have wanted to know more and more about fitness walking and what it can do for them. The World Health Organisation has referred to walking as 'the forgotten art'. Increasing numbers of people throughout the world are now rediscovering for themselves the fitness and weight-loss benefits of regular fitness walking.

This is what walkers have said who have followed our fitness walking plan:

'The walking was excellent. After a week you felt so good, much fitter with endless energy. You wanted to get up in the mornings and get going.' – *Teresa*

'I loved the walking. I had great energy.' – *Julie*

'I was always tired before I started walking.' – *Val*

'I have had more energy. I feel better because I am walking.' – *Barbara*

'Two months ago I could not run up a hill with my grandchildren. I can now. Climbing stairs was difficult. Now it's easy.' – *Beryl*

'I have more energy now than I've ever had.' – *Jan*

And on the subject of *Walking Off Weight*:

'I have seen the pounds come off – more so than with other diets.' – *Val*

'At long last my weight is slowly coming down and I don't feel the restrictions of other diets.' – *Jan*

'I was very overweight. Tried all sorts of diets, but this time the pounds are falling off.' – *Patrick*

This is what the experts have to say about *Walking Off Weight*:

'Walking is my top recommendation for weight loss.' – *Suzanne Beyea*, nurse practitioner, Laconia Clinic, New Hampshire, USA

'Walking is excellent for getting rid of and keeping off weight.' – *Ruth J. Lerner*, PhD, psychologist, Los Angeles, USA

'Walking is a great way to shape up and lose weight without risk of injury.' – *Deepak D. Chabra*, MD, Sacramento, USA

'I recommend walking to all my patients who need to lose weight.' – *Dr Neil Scheffler*, Baltimore Podiatry Group, Maryland, USA

'In our weight-reduction clinic in Beverly Hills we have frequently found walking to help our patients to take off their weight and to keep it off.' – *Howard Flaks*, MD, Beverly Hills, USA

Walking has worked for all these people and their clients and it will work for you.

10 WAYS WALKING WILL WORK FOR YOU

1

WALKING is *a natural, healthy expression of the human body.*
Your body is built for walking – it's the ultimate exercise machine. Walking helps you restore rhythm and balance to your life: it makes you fit, healthy and whole.

2

WALKING is *easy, safe and inexpensive.*
Walking really can't be easier to do – after all, you've been doing it since you were a year old. And it's safe and almost injury-free. All you need is a pair of comfortable walking shoes.

3

WALKING is *aerobic.*
It is the easiest aerobic exercise and will give you all the aerobic benefits of jogging, swimming, aerobics and more extreme exercises – stamina, endurance and cardiovascular fitness.

4

WALKING is *the perfect exercise for weight loss.*
It is the best way to burn calories and increase your body's ability to burn fat. It allows you to work-out longer and burn more total calories than if you were working out too hard with more extreme exercise.

5 WALKING *improves both muscle tone and strength.* It tones and strengthens your hips, thighs, stomach and buttocks and will help your body look sleek and firm. Illustration 1 shows you the main muscle groups used in walking.

6 WALKING is *the best cardiovascular workout.* It conditions the heart: the heart becomes stronger and it pumps more blood with each beat. It needs to do less work, so it lasts longer. Walking lowers blood pressure and raises HDL (good cholesterol).

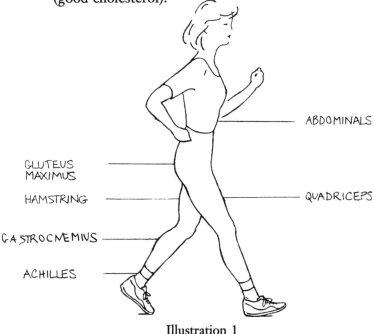

ABDOMINALS

GLUTEUS MAXIMUS

HAMSTRING

QUADRICEPS

GASTROCNEMIUS

ACHILLES

Illustration 1

7 WALKING is *the easiest way for all the family to keep fit.* Why? Because everyone can do it, it's cheap and it's non-competitive. It helps you spend time together – to get fit, lose weight and to talk. The family that walks together talks together.

8

WALKING is *an injury-free way for the over 50s to keep fit.*
Walk longer; live longer. Because walking is a low-stress exercise, almost anyone can begin to walk at any age providing they begin slowly and build up frequency and intensity.

9

WALKING is *the ideal way to relieve stress.*
You will find that the psychological benefits of walking become as important to you as the fitness and weight loss benefits. Walking is an ideal way to relax, to re-energise, to 'burn away' the effects of stress.

10

WALKING *produces a variety of important health benefits.*
Walking can help with back pain, osteoporosis, respiratory problems, diabetes, arthritis, cardiac rehabilitation and a variety of other health problems.

Remember, joggers may start out faster than walkers, but like the hare in Aesop's fable, they start off at a cracking pace and exhaust themselves long before their competitors, while the slower tortoise walks past them to the winning post.

So walk, don't run, to tell your friends and family about the benefits of aerobic fitness walking.

PART ONE

1

WALK SLIM
The Easy Way to Lose a Stone in 30 Days

THE WEIGHT-LOSS WALKOUT

Walking is crucial to every diet plan
DR JAMES RIPPE AND ANN WARD
Exercise Physiology & Nutritional Laboratory, University of Massachusetts

A recent report said that half of all men in Britain are now overweight compared with 39 per cent in 1980 and the proportion of overweight women has increased from 32 per cent to 40 per cent. London Underground trains are being fitted with larger seats to cope with larger people and bed and clothing manufacturers are making design changes in their products. Again, the experts are blaming our sedentary lifestyle and the high fat content in our national diet.

The answer? To eat a low-fat, high-fibre diet based on the healthy food pyramid guidelines suggested by the US Department of Agriculture (USDA) and the World Health Organisation's (WHO) latest advice for healthy eating, and to do moderate aerobic exercise at least three times a week for 20 to 30 minutes. *And the easiest aerobic exercise suggested by all the experts? Walking.*

GETTING STARTED – A STEP BY STEP GUIDE

Walking works because it is a low-stress, moderate exercise. Provided you start slowly and gradually build up your strength and stamina, it is the easiest way to get fit and lose weight.

Research has shown that when you combine a diet with a calorie-burning exercise like aerobic walking you get much better weight loss results. But to keep things simple, all we are asking you to do in the beginning is to walk.

It is much easier to start out exercising and then begin the diet, because walking will get you motivated and keep you motivated. Aerobic exercise gives you more energy and vitality. Remember what the walkers said who followed *The Walking Diet*:

'You wanted to get up in the mornings and get going.' – *Teresa*

'I loved the walking. I had great energy.' – *Julie*

'I have more energy now than I've ever had.' – *Jan*

The only equipment you need is a pair of well-cushioned shoes that give you good support. A training shoe will do the job, either a 'cross-trainer' which is suitable for several sports activities, including walking, or a specialist 'fitness-walking trainer' (see *How to Select a Walking Shoe*). Alternatively, there are now several manufacturers who include cushioning in their shoes similar to that included in a sports training shoe, and styles are available for smart business wear as well as leisure wear. In the USA it's not unusual to see men and women walking briskly from one meeting to another in smart 'business trainers'.

Now you are ready – so let's get out and walk. To begin with you are not going to think about losing weight, technique, or target heart rate. You are not going to worry about your stride or how fast you are going during these first few days. Your first objective is simply to walk.

The easiest way to start walking regularly is simply to walk out of your own front door and do a circuit or a number of circuits round the block and back, or around the local park or another route that is known to you. It is also the easiest way to keep yourself motivated.

You should walk to suit your physical condition. If you are unfit, pregnant or have a diagnosed medical problem which

How to Select a Walking Shoe

WEIGHT – Choose a lightweight design; a walking shoe does not need to absorb as much shock as a running shoe so the midsole cushioning can be reduced to make it lighter.

UPPER CONSTRUCTION – Look for a pliable, soft upper providing good support, and made from a breathable fabric, preferably leather or a design using leather and fabric or mesh.

OUTERSOLE – This is the bottom of the shoe that touches the ground. It should provide durability and should be shock absorbent to protect your feet from bruising. The normal walking motion is to land on your heels and roll your weight forward with a natural rocker motion on to your toes. Some shoes have a rocker profile sole to assist this natural heel-toe motion.

ROOMY TOE-BOX – This should allow the toes room to spread out when they hit the ground and during push off. Toes should be able to move easily up and down and back and forth, and should not feel too tight against any part of the shoe.

FIRM HEEL COUNTER – This is the cup at the back of the inside of the shoe; it wraps around the heel and lends side-to-side support as the heel first makes contact with the ground.

NOTCHED HEEL – This is the padded collar at the back of the shoe in the shape of a notch or a dip to reduce pressure on the heel tendons.

Always buy shoes in the afternoon – your feet tend to swell slightly as the day goes on. When you try shoes on, wear socks that you will be using with the shoes when you walk. To ensure the correct shoe length use the 'thumbnail rule' as a guide. There should be a space the width of your thumbnail between the end of the toe-box and the tip of your longest toe on your longer foot.

will affect your ability to exercise, then check with your doctor before starting to walk briskly.

If you are already fit and active, then you should be able to walk for a minimum of 20 minutes without getting out of breath or becoming tired. Stepping out with a normal stride, in 20 minutes you will cover about a mile (assuming you are walking at 3 mph). Over one week increase your walking speed as you feel comfortable, working towards a goal of a 15-minute mile (4 mph) and increasing your time a few minutes each day until you can walk for 30 minutes comfortably. An easy way to measure walking speed is to count how many steps you take per minute (see *Table 1*). Use this simple conversion table to calculate your speed per hour, which is based on three common stride lengths.

Brisk aerobic walking feels good. Although you are walking faster, once you get into a comfortable stride, the continuous, rhythmic motion of brisk walking is actually easier and less tiring than strolling or slow walking.

Over the next 30 days we are going to convince you just how easy it is to build up a fitness and weight loss programme

Steps per minute			Minutes	Miles
2.0 ft/stride	2.5 ft/stride	3.0 ft/stride	per mile	per hour
90	70	60	30	2
110	90	75	24	2.5
130	105	90	20	3
155	120	105	17	3.5
175	140	120	15	4
200	160	135	13	4.5
220	175	145	12	5

TABLE 1

that works, is fun and that you can do for the rest of your life. Compared with other exercise activities, you are starting out at an advanced level. After all, you have been an accomplished walker since you were a year old.

Walking aerobically helps you slim, burning off around 200 calories every 30 minutes. It speeds up your metabolic rate – the time taken to burn calories – and your raised metabolic rate will continue to burn off calories when exercising is over, helping you to eat well while remaining slim and fit. Combined with a low-fat, high-fibre diet – *The Walk Slim Diet* – walking is the perfect weight management system.

So step out and speed up. What have you got to lose?

YOUR 30-DAY WEIGHT LOSS WALKOUT

Fourteen pounds. You may have more or you may have less to lose. If you're like most people you will have tried many times to lose weight and failed. Now within 30 days you will feel fitter, leaner, more toned up, have more energy than you have ever had and those awkward extra pounds are going to just fall away – they will be history.

Combined with *The Walk Slim Diet* plan, you will have the motivation you need to get going and keep going, not only for 30 days, but for the rest of your life. You are in charge of this weight loss plan. You discover where you are today, then set out to achieve your own goals of fitness and weight loss.

To begin with you need to weigh yourself and measure your height if you don't know it. Then check yourself against the Height/Weight Chart (see *Table 2*). For each height there is an acceptable weight range covering small to large frames. If you are a woman your goal weight should be nearer the lower figure; for men, depending on build, it should be towards the higher end of the scale. This gives you a goal to aim for.

By now you will have been out on several motivating walks and you will be ready to get started with your 30-day plan.

So step out, step it up and walk off those troublesome pounds with your weight loss walkout.

Height without shoes ft in	Small frame st lb	Medium frame st lb	Large frame st lb
HEIGHT/WEIGHT CHART			
WOMEN			
4 10	7 2	7 12	8 7
4 11	7 4	8 0	8 10
5 0	7 7	8 2	8 13
5 1	7 10	8 5	9 2
5 2	7 13	8 7	9 5
5 3	8 2	8 10	9 8
5 4	8 6	9 0	9 12
5 5	8 10	9 5	10 2
5 6	9 0	9 10	10 6
5 7	9 4	10 0	10 10
5 8	9 8	10 5	11 0
5 9	9 12	10 10	11 5
5 10	10 3	11 2	11 10
MEN			
5 3	8 10	9 4	10 0
5 4	8 13	9 7	10 3
5 5	9 2	9 10	10 6
5 6	9 6	10 0	10 10
5 7	9 10	10 4	11 1
5 8	10 0	10 8	11 5
5 9	10 4	10 12	11 9
5 10	10 8	11 2	11 13
5 11	10 12	11 6	12 4
6 0	11 2	11 10	12 8
6 1	11 6	12 0	12 13
6 2	11 10	12 5	13 4
6 3	12 0	12 10	13 9

TABLE 2

YOUR 30-DAY WEIGHT LOSS WALKOUT

DAYS 1–7
Time:
Frequency:
Distance:

30 minutes
5 times a week
1.9 miles

DAYS 8–14
Time:
Frequency:
Distance:

30–40 minutes
5 times a week
1.9–2.5 miles

DAYS 15–21
Time:
Frequency:
Distance:

40–50 minutes
6 times a week
2.5–3.1 miles

DAYS 22–30
Time:
Frequency:
Distance:

50–60 minutes
8 times
3.1–3.75 miles

Okay. You're ready. You've already started walking for up to 30 minutes each day. You are convinced that walking will work for you. You feel better about yourself. You have more energy, you sleep better and when you wake up in the morning you want to get up and get going. You know that all you need to do now is to step out, walk longer and follow *The Walk Slim Diet* and the pounds will start to fall away.

But before you step up to a brisk, regular pace and begin your weight loss walkout you should warm up. Walking is safe and effective because it is a low-impact exercise and it uses muscles which you have been using all your life. Even so, a warm-up improves performance and can help prevent injury by increasing your body temperature with easy rhythmical movements. The following exercises are a balanced combination of limbering, mobility exercises and static stretches to raise the pulse, increase blood flow to the muscles and fluid to the joints, ligaments, tendons and connective tissue.

The warm-up exercises the main muscle groups which you use when you walk – the quadriceps (the large muscle group on the front of the thigh), the hamstrings (the back of the thigh) and the calves and Achilles tendons found at the back of the lower leg from the knee down towards the heel. When these muscles are warmed and relaxed, it becomes easier to get into a good walking rhythm and the muscles can stretch and lengthen more easily to help prevent injury or damage.

Always ease into your stretches using smooth slow movements. You should feel a mild comfortable tension as your body adjusts and eases into the different positions.

Warm Up – Always Start With This

1. SHOULDER LIFTS/CIRCLES
To loosen and relax the neck, shoulders and upper back.

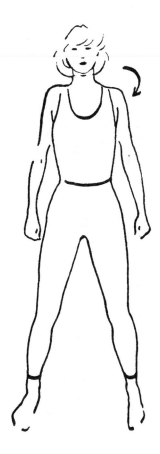

Stand tall with feet hip width apart, knees slightly bent, abdominals pulled in and pelvis tucked under. Relax arms by your sides. Lift and lower shoulders 8 times, rotate shoulders back 8 times and rotate forward 8 times.

2. ARM RAISES
To loosen shoulders and chest.

Stand as above, feet slightly wider than hip width apart. Inhale as you raise arms above head, exhale as you lower arms. Repeat 4 times.

3. KNEE LIFTS

To increase blood flow and oxygen uptake to working muscles, warming up calves, Achilles tendons and quadriceps.

Walk on the spot. Stay tall with abdominals in and a long back. Gradually increase intensity by marching and swinging arms back and forth. Alternatively lift knees up level with your hips so that your thighs are parallel to the floor. Repeat 16 times.

4. QUADRICEP STRETCH (THIGH)
To stretch out quadriceps situated down the front of the thigh.

Using a chair or the wall for balance, stand on left leg with knee slightly bent, pelvis tucked under, trunk upright. Hold on to right foot, keep knees together and ease right heel towards right buttock as the right hip extends gently forwards. Hold for 10–15 seconds. Repeat with other leg.

5. HAMSTRING CURL

To increase circulation and activate and limber hamstring muscles situated on the back of the thigh.

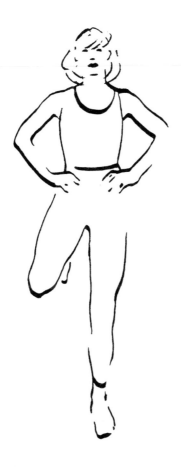

Stand with feet fairly wide apart, toes turned slightly outward, abdominals in, chest up, hands on hips. Lift right heel up and back towards right buttock then lower foot back to floor. Repeat with left foot. Alternate these heel lifts. Deep steady breathing. Repeat 16 times.

6. HAMSTRING STRETCH
To pre-lengthen and prepare muscles behind thigh.

Bend left leg, hands on left thigh. Straighten out right leg in front of you. Point toes, keep knees in line. With a long trunk lean forward slightly lifting chest and holding abdominals in (do not bend from waist). Feel the stretch behind the right thigh in the hamstring muscles as the right leg is lengthened slowly. Hold 10–15 seconds. Repeat on other leg.

7. CALF RAISES
To warm and prepare calf muscles and Achilles tendon.

Stand tall, abdominals in, shoulders back and relaxed, feet together using a wall or chair for balance. Lift heels standing on balls of feet and 'squeeze' into calf muscles. Hold for 2 counts then lower heels down to floor. Repeat 6 times.

8. CALF STRETCH (GASTROCNEMIUS)
To stretch out main body of calf.

Facing and resting hands on wall – head up, back straight, abdominals in – place right foot in front of left with right foot approximately 6 inches from wall. Both heels remain flat on the floor, toes pointing forwards, as you ease pelvis forward to feel stretch in main body of left calf. Hold 10–15 seconds.

9. LOWER CALF STRETCH (SOLEUS) AND ACHILLES

To stretch out lower calf and Achilles tendon.

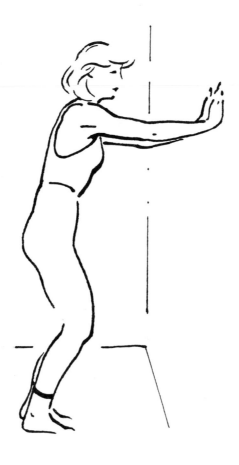

Face and place hands on wall as in previous stretch. This time keep feet together approximately 2 feet from wall. Toes forward and heels down. Keeping hips tucked in, gently bend knees until stretch is felt in lower calf and Achilles tendon.

10. ANKLE RELEASE

Holding on to wall, lift one foot. Bend supporting leg. Slowly rotate foot one way then the other. Repeat on other foot.

Once you have done your warm-up exercises, the best way to continue warming up is to walk. Start gradually, building your pace over 4 or 5 minutes, allowing your heart beat to rise by walking at a brisk comfortable pace. Walk for 30 minutes each day during this first week.

Over the next 30 days you are going to gradually increase your walking time from 30 minutes a day up to 40, 50 then 60 minutes. You are going to walk 5 times each week and in weeks 3 and 4 you are going to increase this to 6 times a week. Starting out walking around 2 miles a day, by the end of 30 days you will be walking nearly 4 miles each day. And the pounds will be just falling off.

Cooldown/Post-exercise Stretches

A cooldown after aerobic walking is as important as a warm-up beforehand. Don't just stop walking – gently reduce your pace over several minutes as you finish your walk. This will help you to avoid sore muscles and will return your heart and blood pressure back to a normal level. End your walkout with a few cooldown stretches.

1. STANDING SHOULDER STRETCH
To ease and stretch muscles around the shoulder.

Stand tall, feet hip width apart, knees slightly bent, bottom tucked under (pelvis tilted forward to prevent lower back from arching). Clasp hands together, breathe easy, pull in abdominals and extend arms up above head. Hold for 4 counts, rest and repeat.

2. STANDING CHEST STRETCH
To stretch across front of chest.

Stand as above, adopting pelvic tilt and keeping shoulders down and relaxed. Clasp hands together behind back. Slowly extend and lengthen arms as you lift up behind back. Hold for 4 counts, rest and repeat.

REPEAT FOLLOWING STRETCHES AS IN WARM-UP PHASE:

4.	Quadricep stretch	*Fig 4*
5.	Hamstring stretch	*Fig 6*
6.	Calf stretch	*Fig 8*
7.	Achilles stretch	*Fig 9*

Muscles shorten and tighten when you walk, so these stretches will allow the muscles to return to their original length.

DAYS 8–14 STEP TO IT

You are now making progress. You should be getting into your stride and a good walking rhythm and you should be starting to see the pounds fall away. This week you are going to gradually increase your daily walking time from 30 to 40 minutes and you are going to think about the way you walk – your posture, stride length, heel-toe motion and breathing. You are going to think tall and walk tall and note how your body feels in contact with the ground. You are going to feel the rhythm in your feet, calves, thighs, arms and shoulders. And you're going to let go – and relax.

Posture Perfect

Walk straight.
Aesop's Fables, 600BC

As you walk along the road look at other people. Notice how many are slouched, their shoulders hunched and rounded. Notice how many have their heads down, seeming to move almost in a world of their own, unaware of others. They seem to shuffle rather than walk. What does this suggest to you?

Now look at yourself. The way that you walk says a lot about you to other people and it tells you a lot about yourself. So think about your posture and walk naturally. Good posture helps you tone your body; it improves oxygen and blood circulation; and it helps to prevent injuries, particularly as you start to walk faster than normal.

Good posture helps you feel more alert and in command of the situation. And you will feel more positive and have more energy to get where you are going. Good posture gives your body a natural walking rhythm and sense of balance and you can walk for longer without tiring.

Here are some posture pointers and fitness walking techniques:

- WALK TALL – As you step out, your back should be straight and the weight of your body should be slightly in front of your ankles, not back on your heels. Pull in your stomach and flatten the small of your back by tucking in your buttocks under your spine – the pelvic tilt. Walk tall with your head level and eyes focused straight ahead (not looking down). Your shoulders should be level and relaxed.

- LAND ON YOUR HEELS, PUSH OFF YOUR TOES – As you walk, push off with the ball and toes of your back foot and land in the middle of your front heel; then continue with a heel-toe rolling motion. This motion holds and supports your whole body. You walk tall from your heels upwards – the Chinese say that 'the true man breathes with his heels'.

- MAKE YOUR STRIDE LONG – Take the longest stride that is comfortable, leading with your hips, letting your arms swing naturally in opposition to your legs (right arm forward with left leg), and keeping your elbows close in to your sides. If you relax your shoulders, then your arms will swing by themselves, finding their own natural rhythm. As you walk faster, you will find that your arms bend naturally and quicken up to keep pace with your legs. Your hands should be softly closed, not clenched and tensed. Striding will loosen your hips, making them more flexible and it will tighten your lower abdominal muscles, giving you a stronger, flatter stomach. Think hips and thighs – fat goodbye!

- YOUR WALKING CENTRE – Imagine a straight line going down the road between the centre of your feet and stretching ahead of you. This represents your walking centre. Keep your legs parallel to this line and your toes pointed directly ahead and walk with your normal stride. Regular, rhythmic walking in this way can have a beneficial psychological and meditational effect upon you, and help you to centre yourself within your own personal space.

- BREATHE NATURALLY – As you increase pace, breathe naturally and inhale and exhale rhythmically through the nose. Try abdominal breathing. This is used by singers, meditators and athletes and can double the volume of air you inhale with each breath. To breathe deeply, inhale by first moving your abdomen outwards. You will feel your stomach rise, then your upper abdomen, and finally your chest. Then breathe out by letting your stomach relax. Take one breath per step, or as you walk faster, one breath every two steps.

DAYS 15–21 STEP IT UP

This week you are going to step up your daily walk time from 40 to 50 minutes, you are going to walk one extra day and you are going to think about all the different ways you can knock up those extra miles. You don't have to do all your walking in one session. Many of you will not be able to find the time during the week to do this, so let's look at all the ways where you can fit in those extra weight-loss miles. Try not to walk for less than 20 minutes at one session, as it takes several minutes to warm-up and to get into a good walking stride and once you get going it's easier to keep going. Think about all those calories that you are losing – around 200 for every 30 minutes walking, and up to a few hundred more when you finish walking due to your increased metabolic rate.

When and Where to Walk

- *Walk in the morning* – This is a good time to prepare your mind and body for the day ahead: a quiet time to think and make plans to give you a physical and psychological boost for the day.

- *Walk to work* – If it's practical, this is one way of fitting in all those weight-loss miles each week. If your work-place is too far, walk to the bus or train station. Try getting off the bus or train a stop early on your way to work or returning home from work and walk the rest of the way.

- *Park further away* – Whenever you take the car, either to work or shopping, park a distance away from your destination and walk the rest of the way.

- *Walk in your lunch hour* – This is one way to get outdoors and re-charge yourself for the afternoon. A brisk aerobic walk will lift your energy and vitality and will give you the 'zip' you need to get you through the rest of the day. Take a friend or friends with you.

- *Walk the stairs* – Use the stairs instead of a lift. Stair climbing tones the legs and builds cardiovascular fitness and you can walk away up to twice as many calories as normal aerobic walking.

- *Walk in the evening* – This is a time to relax and ease away the stress after a busy day. Evening walks are a time to reflect on the passing day; a time to let go; a time to try 'walking meditation' (*see Chapter 4*).

- *Walk with the family* – Walking is an opportunity to spend more time together with those you love most. Walk together; take the kids; take grandma; take the dog. Walking together helps you to talk together and spend more quality time with each other.

- *Start a walking group* – At home or at work get a few friends together and walk regularly. It will help to keep you motivated and give you a chance to talk.

- *Take a walking holiday* – Once walking becomes part of your life you will want to go on walking holidays or on a hiking trip in the countryside.

- *Walk with the weather* – Don't let the weather put you off walking. Dress suitably and enjoy the changing face of the seasons. Each season has its own special pleasures to offer the observant walker.

DAYS 22–30 JUST STEPS AWAY

For your final nine days you will increase your walk time gradually from 50 to 60 minutes and you will walk for 8 of those days. Remember to vary your routine with morning walks, work-break walks, lunchtime walks, late afternoon walks and evening walks. Persuade a friend to walk with you or get the family out for a walk. You are also going to think this week about the best speed to walk at for cardiovascular health (how to build a strong heart and lungs).

Day 30 – congratulations, you've made it! You should feel proud of yourself. You have kept up your motivation. You should be fitter, slimmer, have more energy and you should want to continue walking for the rest of your life. In future, if you put on a few extra pounds you will be able to just walk them away.

Target Heart Rate – Is It Necessary?

What has all this to do with weight loss? Well, it's true that walking will burn away the calories however fast you walk, but generally speaking a brisk aerobic walk between 3.5 to 4.0 mph will burn more calories, more quickly and more efficiently. The key thing is getting into a rhythm – your rhythm, one that works for you.

And remember, no matter how you measure it, when you walk aerobically, you are not only getting weight loss benefits, but also cardiovascular benefits (stronger heart and lungs) and benefits to your fitness and long term health.

Walking can be aerobic, even without checking your pulse and measuring target heart rate. However, this simple technique ensures that you are walking within your aerobic 'heart training zone' and it is simple and safe.

You need to walk intensely enough to raise your heart beat between 60 per cent and 80 per cent of its maximum. (For the very unfit 50 per cent to 60 per cent is an adequate goal.) Work out your ideal pulse rate (called target heart rate) this way:

1. Subtract your age from 220. If you are 40 then that will be 220–40 = 180. That's your maximum heart rate.
2. Now calculate 60 per cent and 80 per cent of your maximum heart rate: 180 × .60 = 108 and 180 × .80 = 144.

   Your goal when walking is to keep your pulse between 108 and 144 beats per minute. Get into a good walking rhythm, say for five minutes or so, then check your pulse at the carotid artery in your neck, or at your wrist. Looking at your watch's second hand count the beats for 6 seconds then multiply by 10 – that's your pulse.

YOUR TARGET HEART RATE

AGE	MAXIMUM HEART RATE	60% LEVEL	80% LEVEL
20	200	120	160
25	195	117	156
30	190	114	152
35	185	111	148
40	180	108	144
45	175	105	140
50	170	102	136
55	165	99	132
60	160	96	128
65	155	93	124
70	150	90	120

TABLE 3

If you are below the lower end of your target range, then speed up a bit to bring yourself within it. If you are above the higher end of your target range, then slow down until you are back within your target zone. If you find measuring your pulse on the move difficult, then measure it immediately you end your work out and adjust your effort next time out. You can use this simple table to work out your upper and lower target limits.

Don't let pulse taking take the fun out of your walking. Once you become experienced, you will be able to keep within your target zone simply by knowing how it 'feels'. One way to know how it 'feels' or how you 'perceive' it, is to use the following Rating of Perceived Exertion, or RPE:

RPE: Rating of Perceived Exertion	
Maximum Exertion	20
Extremely Hard	19
	18
Very Hard	17
	16
Hard	15
	14
Somewhat Hard	13
	12
Light	11
	10
Very Light	9
	8
Extremely Light	7
None	6

TABLE 4

The RPE relies more on your feeling, or gut sense, of how hard you are exercising. It works on the assumption that if you think you are getting a hard workout, then you probably are, and your heart rate is likely to be in the aerobic target zone.

The RPE runs from 6 to 20. Each number represents a

phase that describes your perception of how hard you are exercising. Six, for example, means 'no exertion'; 20 means 'maximum exertion'. By adding a zero to each number, you get a rough approximation of heart rate. For instance, an RPE of 12–13 represents a workout which is 'somewhat hard' in the target heart range of 120–130.

The RPE is a rough guide only and converting it to a heart rate is difficult for older people and for those out of condition. For older people, the maximum heart rate is much lower, and for those out of condition, even moderate exercise can set their heart racing. But studies show that the RPE scale represents a close relationship between a person's perceived exertion during exercise and heart rate.

Instead of using target heart rate or RPE, an easy guide to effectiveness is to walk at a speed which will leave you slightly breathless but still able to carry on a conversation. For most people this will be a speed between 3.5 mph and 4 mph. This should be sufficient to achieve an aerobic workout and develop a healthy heart.

*More than 90 per cent of people who lose weight on diets put
the weight back on again*

Most diets are temporary solutions to a permanent problem
– which is how to lose weight and maintain that weight loss.
Most diets fail because:

- on their own, without exercising, you lose weight rapidly
  and much of this is lean tissue, not fat.

- your metabolism slows down – your body thinks it's being
  starved so it conserves fat, the opposite of what you want!

- they are extreme, impractical and simply boring.

With some slimming foods offering miracle weight loss
without exercising, and some fitness plans offering quick
weight loss without dieting, it's easy to see why some people
think that you can diet without exercising or exercise without
dieting.

But the answer is not that simple.

If you want to get fit, lose weight and maintain your fitness
and weight loss for the rest of your life, then you need to
diet and exercise. Most people fail on diets because the diets are
temporary (the yo-yo syndrome), unpleasant and nutritionally
unsound – and the exercise suggested is often difficult to keep
up and boring. The diets leave you feeling deprived, bad
tempered, depressed and yes – hungry!

But don't despair. New research now shows that adding
exercise to a moderate diet is a far more effective way to
lose weight than dieting alone. According to researchers at
Stanford University Medical School, Stanford, California,
USA, combining a walking programme with a healthy diet
results in a greater loss of total body fat and dangerous blood
cholesterol than dieting alone. Exercisers in the Stanford
study lost almost double the percentage of body fat than those
who only dieted.

Moderation is the key to successful dieting and exercise.

Moderate exercise (brisk, aerobic walking) with a moderate diet plan (*The Walk Slim Diet*) is the easiest and quickest way to lose those unwanted pounds and keep them off forever. Aerobic walking works because it speeds up your metabolic rate (performance level) and burns fat, not lean tissue. Aerobic walking works because it is an exercise that you can keep up for the rest of your life. When it comes to achieving results, aerobic walking is simply the best.

The World Health Organisation (WHO) recently published worldwide scientific research recommending the amount and type of food we should eat. The key to both healthy eating and weight loss is to revamp your eating habits – eating more complex carbohydrates, fruit and vegetables and cutting down on fat, sugar and salt.

Sounds simple? It works. And to add to the growing debate on healthy eating, the US Department of Agriculture (USDA) has released its Food Guide Pyramid (see page 54) which makes similar recommendations to the WHO guidelines on healthy eating.

The message that comes across loud and clear is that we should eat fat sparingly. We used to think that if we ate 3,500 calories more than we needed then we would gain a pound, whatever the source of those calories. Recent research, though, has overthrown this idea. It now seems that the body is more efficient at making body fat from dietary fats than from proteins and carbohydrates. Put simply – it's the fat in our diet that makes us fat. We now know that:

---

each fat gram we eat contains 9 calories

each carbohydrate gram we eat contains 4 calories

And this is only part of the story. For every carbohydrate calorie we eat, the body uses up more than 25 per cent of those calories just to digest, absorb, transport and store the calories internally. But for each fat calorie you eat, only 3 per cent is used up to convert it internally. Our bodies burn carbohydrates and store fats.

And that's not all. Those same fats are also raising your cholesterol level, damaging your blood vessels and possibly contributing to cancers and other degenerative diseases.

The good news, though, is that you don't have to count calories with *The Walk Slim Diet*. All you need to do is to focus on those foods in the healthy food pyramid which will lower your fat intake and increase your carbohydrates.

So forget past diets. This diet is simple, easy to keep up and it works. So step to it and eat healthily.

Four Easy Steps to Lose a Stone in 30 Days

STEP 1 WALK TO WIN

Brisk fitness walking is an aerobic exercise. If you walk in the low to moderate range of your target heart rate, you will burn stored fat as fuel after the first 20 minutes. And the longer you walk, the more fat you will burn.

Compared with being sedentary (sitting at a desk, watching TV) you will burn around five times as many calories when you walk aerobically at 3.5–4 mph and on average you will lose up to 200 calories every 30 minutes.

During aerobic walking the heart and respiratory rates increase and your metabolism (performance level) speeds up. Metabolism is the process where food, as fuel, is broken down and, with the help of oxygen, is 'burnt off' and converted into heat and energy. Many dieters use the excuse of not being able to do anything about their metabolism, but in fact metabolism can be altered by the type of food you eat and the exercise you take.

It is the extra oxygen provided by aerobic – 'with air' – walking and higher metabolic rate that burns off the excess calories and keeps them off forever. And that's not all.

Try walking first thing in the morning before you have eaten. Research shows that if you want to lose weight then this is the best time, because glycogen reserves are very low in the morning so energy is obtained by using body fat.

Glycogen is a form of carbohydrate stored in the muscles and liver. When you first start out walking, a major part of the energy provided is drawn from your glycogen pool. But as you continue to walk you begin to draw energy from your fat stores. So the lower your glycogen level the sooner you will start to pull on these fat stores and lose weight.

Try the appetite-suppressing powers of walking and walk before meals. Don't be concerned about your appetite increasing with walking. It is only very vigorous exercise that tends to increase appetite. As long as you walk at a moderate pace (around 70 per cent of your target heart rate) then you should feel less hungry than you would if you did no exercise at all.

Try walking after meals. Not a brisk aerobic walk – just a short, relaxed stroll. It will help digestion, relieve that bloated feeling and give you renewed energy to get on with the rest of the day. Research carried out by Bryant Stamford, PhD, exercise physiologist and director of the Health Promotion Center at the University of Louisville, USA, suggests that a moderate workout right after a meal gives you a fat-burning bonus. Whereas a 30-minute pre-meal walk would burn up around 200 calories plus a fraction from the 'afterburn effect' – the tendency to continue burning calories after the walk is over – a 30-minute post-meal walk could burn another 15 per cent of the total.

So the first step is to get outside and walk to win.

STEP 2 INCREASE CC FOODS

A well-balanced diet is the key to health, vitality and successful weight control. British and US government guidelines are now urging us to reduce our fat consumption and balance this by eating more CC foods (complex carbohydrates – bread, potatoes, cereals, pasta and rice) and more fruit and vegetables.

All over the world the people least likely to suffer from certain cancers and heart disease are those whose diets are rich in plant food – starchy CC foods, fruit and vegetables. The good news for slimmers is that the same diet is also the best way to lose weight and keep it off. So eating more CC

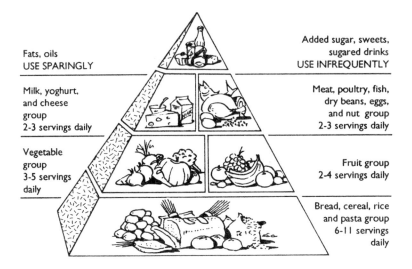

Fats, oils
USE SPARINGLY

Added sugar, sweets,
sugared drinks
USE INFREQUENTLY

Milk, yoghurt,
and cheese
group
2-3 servings daily

Meat, poultry, fish,
dry beans, eggs,
and nut group
2-3 servings daily

Vegetable
group
3-5 servings
daily

Fruit group
2-4 servings daily

Bread, cereal, rice
and pasta group
6-11 servings
daily

foods and more fruit and vegetables is the quickest, easiest and best way to lose weight and eat healthily.

The healthy food pyramid (above) shows the main food groups at a glance. The idea is to eat most of the foods at the base of the pyramid and least of the foods at the top, eating at least the minimum number of servings suggested on each level and using fats, oils and sweets sparingly.

Making permanent changes in your own and your family's eating habits is the key to success and the diet pyramid shows you what to do. Don't think in terms of foods being good or bad; simply as foods to increase and decrease. This means giving a higher profile to some foods rather than others.

The pyramid highlights the key action areas for a balanced diet. At the base of the pyramid are the CC foods: bread, potatoes, cereals, pasta and rice. These are the foods you need most of, so build your meals around them. Fruit and vegetables form the next level of the pyramid and you should eat at least 5–9 servings daily. *The Walk Slim Diet* provides most of your daily energy intake from CC foods and fruit and vegetables on the first two levels of the pyramid.

Moving up the pyramid, you can add protein in the form of fish and seafood, and you can add moderate amounts of white meat – chicken and turkey. Foods towards the top of the pyramid should play a reducing role in a low-fat nutritious diet. Red meat is higher in fat than white meat, and dairy products are all high in fat so use them sparingly. Watch out for 'added' sugar in the form of sweets, sugared drinks, cakes and biscuits.

Remember, it's the fat in your diet that makes you fat. So cut down on it and try using low fat substitutes:

INSTEAD OF:	USE:
full-fat milk	skimmed or semi-skimmed milk
butter and lard	low-fat margarine or spread
cream	natural yogurt or reduced fat cream
cream- or cheese-based sauces	tomato- or yogurt-based sauces
salad dressing or mayonnaise	lemon juice, lime juice or reduced calorie mayonnaise
desserts	fresh fruit or low fat yogurt
biscuits, cakes and crisps	fresh fruit or crudités

STEP 3 STOCK CHECK – RECHARGE YOUR SHOPPING LIST

Make your shopping lists for *The Walk Slim Diet* from the following:

GREENGROCER'S LIST

apples	pears	bananas
lemons	limes	grapefruit
oranges	tangerines	grapes
melon – Cantaloup	peaches	nectarines
Galia	papaya	mango
Piel de Sapo	pineapple	kiwi fruit
watermelon	figs	dates
raspberries	strawberries	blackberries
blueberries	redcurrants	rhubarb
onions	garlic	leeks
potatoes	carrots	parsnips
beans – broad	turnips	swede
French	Brussels sprouts	cabbage
runner	cauliflower	spinach
peas	mangetout	sweetcorn
peppers – red	courgettes	aubergines
green	mushrooms	fennel
herbs – basil	tomatoes	cucumber
parsley	celery	celeriac
dill	beetroot	chicory
mint	lettuce	watercress

FISHMONGER'S LIST

oily fish – tuna	white fish – haddock
salmon	cod
sardines	monkfish
kippers	sole
herrings	plaice
mackerel	hake
	swordfish
shellfish – prawns	coley
crab	whiting
lobster	

BUTCHER'S LIST

white meat – chicken
    chicken breast
      fillets
    turkey breast
      fillets
    turkey mince
lean red meat – lamb steaks
    sirloin or
    fillet steaks

pork fillet

game – venison
    rabbit
    guinea fowl

GROCER'S LIST

bread – wholemeal
    pitta
pasta (wholemeal if possible)
    – spaghetti
    penne
    rigatoni
rice – brown
    white
    risotto
seeds – pumpkin
    sunflower
    sesame
nuts – chestnuts
    almonds
    walnuts
spices – coriander
    cumin
    chilli
    turmeric
milk (skimmed or semi-skimmed)
low fat yogurt
low fat margarine

Nam Pla fish sauce (available from Oriental foodshops)

chopped tomatoes
tomato purée
tinned tuna in brine
tinned salmon
anchovies
baked beans
red kidney beans
butter beans
soya beans
lentils
corn or sunflower oil
olive oil
white wine vinegar
sultanas
raisins
sweetcorn
petits pois
dried mixed herbs
cereals
eggs
low fat cottage cheese
reduced calorie mayonnaise
Lo-salt
mineral water
soy sauce
Tabasco or chilli sauce

The Walk Slim Diet, based on the healthy eating pyramid, is the easiest way to weight loss without counting calories. The recipes based on low-fat, high-fibre foods are easy to follow and quick to prepare. They are nutritious and offer a balanced diet either for an individual or the whole family.

The Walk Slim Diet gives you a 30-day plan of light meals and main meals (page numbers are included and the recipes can be found in Chapter 6). With each recipe, serve fresh vegetables and/or a salad – in the food pyramid we suggest that you eat 3–5 portions of vegetables every day. A further source of fibre is wholemeal bread which makes a satisfying addition to a meal. Finish with fresh fruit, or eat fruit as a snack during the day: 2–4 pieces of fruit each day are recommended in the food pyramid. If you prefer to substitute some recipes in the 30-day plan then make your choice from the recipes in Chapter 6, balancing the meat, fish and vegetarian meals within each week.

You can choose whether you want the main meal or light meal at lunch time or in the evening. If you are out at work all day, you may wish to take your light meal with you. Many of the light meals can be put into a food container. A salad pocketed in pitta bread makes an appetising light meal. If you are making up a lunch box, add a few crudités (raw vegetables such as carrots, celery and red or green peppers cut into slices), a low fat yogurt and some fresh fruit for a satisfying meal. For young children, prepare the fruit, such as cutting an orange into segments and putting in a food bag, as it is much easier for them to cope with and far less is wasted.

The Walk Slim breakfast

Many nutritionists agree that breakfast is the most important meal of the day. If you are trying to lose weight, and skip breakfast, you will probably be tempted into overeating later in the day – a good breakfast can help to prevent this. And it has been shown that people who have breakfast work more efficiently than those who make do with a cup of tea or coffee to start the day. Porridge is a good source of energy and is very satisfying. Tomatoes, mushrooms or baked beans with wholemeal toast make an excellent low-fat breakfast. Fruit is very refreshing, is low in fat and can be a good source of fibre – for example, 4 ounces of prunes contain 8 grams of fibre. As a change from eating them on their own, try making a dried fruit salad.

Fish is a rich source of vitamins and minerals. Kippers and smoked haddock are traditional breakfast foods and make an appetising and nourishing meal.

Eggs are an excellent food, but cook them without extra fat. A poached or boiled egg with wholemeal toast is very nourishing. And a scrambled egg or an omelette cooked in a non-stick pan and served with some fresh bread makes a good breakfast.

Fruit and vegetables freshly juiced provide immediate energy. A glass first thing in the morning gives instant vitality and a feeling of well-being. Juices contain vital vitamins and minerals and they are quickly assimilated by the body. Try different combinations of fruit and vegetable juices – a good juice to start with is carrot mixed with apple.

Entertaining

If you are entertaining, use a Walk Slim main-meal recipe and, as a first course, serve one of the light-meal recipes such as Smoked Fish Pâté, Chicken with Mango or one of the salads. A fresh fruit platter makes a lovely dessert – choose 3 or 4 different fruits, slice or cut as appropriate, and arrange on a serving plate, garnished with a sprig of mint. It is appetising, nutritious and low in fat as well as being delicious to eat.

The Walk Slim Diet

DAY	LIGHT MEAL	MAIN MEAL
1	Garden Salad (p 124)	Chicken Provençal (p 153)
2	Curried Potatoes and Petits Pois (p 127)	Baked Fish with Toasted Almonds (p 148)
3	Tuscan Salad (p 121)	Sweet and Sour Courgettes and Peppers (p 143)
4	Egg Mayonnaise with Prawns and Grapes (p 132)	Mexican Turkey (p 158)
5	Tuna and Leek Salad (p 128)	Vegetable Pilau (p 141)
6	Chicken with Mango (p 123)	Pasta with Smoked Salmon (p 138)
7	Red Cabbage and Apple Mayonnaise (p 125)	Turkish Lamb (p 160)
8	Italian Salad (p 118)	Bean Ragoût (p 145)
9	Carrot and Tuna with Oranges (p 123)	Chicken Val Bon (p 154)
10	Mushroom and Pepper Omelette (p 132)	White Fish with Tomatoes and Peas (p 149)
11	Mediterranean Salad (p 122)	Pasta Amatriciana (p 137)
12	Tomato and Olive Crostini (p 136)	Cantonese Chicken (p 156)
13	Mexican Prawns (p 118)	Daube d'Aubergines (p 146)
14	Vegetable Kebabs (p 131)	Pork in Red Wine (p 159)
15	Spanish Salad (p 119)	Ratatouille (p 145)

The Walk Slim Diet

DAY	LIGHT MEAL	MAIN MEAL
16	Avocado with Orange (p 134)	Prawns with Rice (p 142)
17	Watercress and Bean Salad (p 126)	Tropical Chicken (p 157)
18	Mangetout and Ham Omelette (p 132)	Vegetable Goulash (p 146)
19	Russian Salad (p 127)	Turkey Koftas (p 157)
20	Aubergine with Mozzarella (p 131)	White Fish with Leeks (p 148)
21	Stuffed Tomatoes (p 130)	Beef with Peppers (p 161)
22	Spring Salad (p 124)	Pasta with Tuna and Walnuts (p 138)
23	Marinated Courgettes and Mushrooms (p 122)	Normandy Chicken (p 153)
24	Pepper Salad (p 119)	Prawn Korma (p 150)
25	Salmon, Apple and Cashew Nuts (p 120)	Pasta Siciliana (p 137)
26	Mangetout with Red Pepper (p 125)	Fish with Pine Nuts and Sultanas (p 150)
27	Eggs Florentine (p 129)	Scampi Provençal (p 151)
28	Ham and Cheese Crostini (p 136)	Lamb with Courgettes (p 161)
29	Chicory and Tuna with Kiwi Fruit (p 123)	Spicy Vegetables (p 144)
30	Pasta and Bean Salad (p 125)	Moroccan Chicken (p 155)

Radical Advice –
Step Up on A C E Foods

Experts have long suspected that there is a link between cancer, heart disease and diet and 35 per cent of all cancers are now thought to be linked to diet. Cancer and heart disease are thought to start with damage to cells caused by 'free radicals', destructive by-products of oxygen which attack our blood vessels and vital organs causing irreversible cell damage. Vitamin C, vitamin E and beta-carotene, a form of vitamin A, can protect against cancer and heart disease by eliminating free radicals. These vital vitamins are known as anti-oxidants or free radical scavengers and they mop up the destructive reactions caused by free radicals.

Leading government health agencies now advise that the best protection against cancer and heart disease is to eat more foods rich in the 'ACE' vitamins. ACE vitamins are found in the following:

Beta-carotene:	dark green leafy vegetables, yellow and orange vegetables and fruits such as spinach, broccoli, peas, cress, asparagus, carrots, sweet potatoes, tomatoes, apricots, peaches, cherries, mangoes, cantaloup melon
Vitamin C:	citrus fruit, strawberries, blackcurrants, kiwi fruit, raw cabbage, green leafy vegetables, green peppers, potatoes, swedes, parsnips, tomatoes
Vitamin E:	nuts, seeds, whole grains, soya beans, vegetable oils especially sunflower oil, fish liver oils, green leafy vegetables

Three good portions of vegetables and two of fruit each day is the best way to ensure that you get enough of the 'ACE' vitamins.

Doctors at Harvard Medical School also believe that anti-oxidants present in beta-carotene may reduce the effects of LDL, or 'bad cholesterol'.

Cutting Cholesterol

Cholesterol is a fatty substance that is found naturally in all human and animal tissues. Manufactured in the liver, cholesterol is essential to a number of body processes such as the metabolism of fat and the formation of hormones. Most of the cholesterol in the bloodstream is made in the body, but some foods which we eat contain cholesterol (dietary cholesterol).

Cholesterol is carried in the bloodstream by special proteins called lipoproteins. They come in two types – high density lipoproteins (HDLs) and low density (LDLs). HDLs are sometimes called 'good' and LDLs 'bad' cholesterol. The higher your HDL level the lower the risk of heart disease.

You can affect your total cholesterol level by reducing your intake of saturated fat. This is found in fatty meat products (pies and sausages), full fat dairy foods, biscuits and cakes. High cholesterol foods include shellfish, eggs, offal and dairy foods.

The best way to lower total cholesterol and to boost HDL levels is to make lifestyle changes – particularly diet and exercise. Follow *The Walk Slim Diet* by cutting saturated fat and eating more complex carbohydrates, fruit, vegetables, fish and white meat. And walk aerobically at least 4 times a week for 30 minutes at a time.

Stay Slim Forever

Using *The Walk Slim Diet*, you will easily be able to lose 3 to 4 pounds a week until you get back to your goal weight. Then it's simply a matter of following the rules of healthy eating and walking a minimum of 4 times a week for 30 minute at an aerobic rate to maintain your weight and long term fitness.

Work up a sweat once a day
– Spartan Saying, circa 430 BC

Aerobic walking will give you stamina and endurance (aerobic fitness), a strong heart and lungs, develop your lower body and tone some of your upper body muscles, but it cannot provide all the exercise you need for whole body fitness. Whole body fitness requires stamina, strength and suppleness, and performing the exercises in the Whole-Body Workout three times a week will help provide you with this:

STAMINA – As you improve your stamina you increase the efficiency of your cardiovascular system: your heart and circulatory system. As the heart muscle becomes stronger and more efficient, it beats at a slower, more powerful rate, giving it less work to do in everyday life. These stamina building exercises are additional to the stamina that walking gives you.

STRENGTH – These exercises involve the repeated action of muscles against resistance. Regular local exercise is needed for the development and maintenance of good muscle tone, strength and endurance, giving you the ability to sustain prolonged activity without becoming tired. Stronger muscles mean that you can lift and carry with greater ease.

SUPPLENESS – Suppleness is about flexibility. Good flexibility will enable you to use your muscles and joints throughout the full potential range of movement – to bend, reach, twist and turn with ease. After an initial warm-up, the best way to stretch a muscle is through a relaxed sustained stretch and not by forcing or bouncing your body into any position. Always stretch within your own capabilities – never stretch to the point of pain. The stretch should be applied gradually. Ease into the hold position and remain relaxed. A mild tension should be felt – this should decrease as you hold.
Stretching is performed at two different levels. The *easy*

stretch, included in the warm-up, is used to pre-lengthen and prepare the muscles for work. The *developmental stretch*, included in the cool-down, involves holding your static stretch for longer to help improve flexibility and range of movement.

Walking is a moderate exercise which allows you to build up to an aerobic level without straining yourself. Similarly, these exercises have all been designed to help you build stamina, strength and suppleness without straining yourself. The number of repetitions and the length of time that exercises are held is only a guide – if necessary, reduce them to what you find comfortable.

As an individual your level of fitness is unique. If you are unfit or overweight and have poor muscle tone and flexibility, then you must progress gradually with the exercises. You should never feel pain. Your movements should flow naturally. Never force – keep within your own ability, learn to listen to your body and you will not go far wrong.

Whole-body fitness allows you to do the things you want to do when you want to do them. And it helps you control your weight, ease away stress, sleep better, feel more confident about yourself and look better, too.

1. BOX PUSH UPS
To strengthen arms and chest.

On all fours, place hands directly under shoulders, fingers facing forward. Pull in abdominals and tilt pelvis to straighten back. Keep hips placed above your knees as you bend elbows lowering your forehead to the floor then push up straightening arms without locking into the elbow joints, or rounding shoulders. Keep the movement smooth with the head in line with the spine. 2–3 sets of 8.

2. SHOULDER STRETCH
To ease upper arm and shoulders.

From all fours, gently sit back over heels, keeping buttocks just above heels. Extend arms along the floor in front of you. Relax your head down and press palms into floor. Hold. Lengthen arms slightly more. Press palms again. Hold 10–15 seconds.

3. TRICEPS STRETCH
To stretch and tone triceps.

Sit tall on floor, hold abdominals in and lengthen spine, legs in a comfortable position in front of you. Raise arms, bend right elbow. Rest right hand on upper back. Hold just above right elbow with left hand. Slowly lift head up and ease back against right arm until you feel a stretching sensation in the back of right arm. Hold 6 seconds. Repeat other side.

4. HIP/OUTER THIGH LIFTS
To strengthen and tone hip and outer thigh.

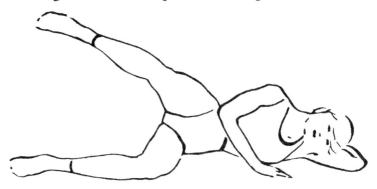

Lie on side with hips, shoulders and head in a straight line. Bend both knees to a 90 degree angle keeping them in line with your hips. Relax and let the upper body weight naturally fall forward. Hold abdominals in, back straight and top hip pressed forward. Lift and lower top leg, keeping knees in line, one above the other. Squeeze into outer thigh and hip as you lift. Repeat on other leg.

5. INNER THIGH
To strengthen and tone inner thigh muscles.

Lying on your side, as in *Fig 4*, from both knees bent, slowly extend out and straighten lower leg in line with the upper body. Keeping the upper leg bent and relaxed forward, slowly lift and lower bottom leg a few inches with the inside of your leg and foot facing the ceiling. Repeat 10 times. Repeat on other leg.

6. SPINAL/OUTER THIGH STRETCH

To stretch lower back, outer thigh, hip and neck.

Lie on back, both knees bent, feet on floor. Gently drop both legs to one side as you extend both arms from chest level and lower to other side. Look towards your hands to release your neck. Hold 5–10 seconds. Slowly lift knees and arms to centre. Repeat other side.

7. INNER THIGH STRETCH
To release inner thighs.

Lie on your back, knees bent, hold abdominals in towards small of back and press back into floor to prevent arching. Keep feet together as you slowly let the knees part and legs open towards floor. Relax and hold 5–10 seconds.

8. PELVIC TILT
To strengthen abdominals.

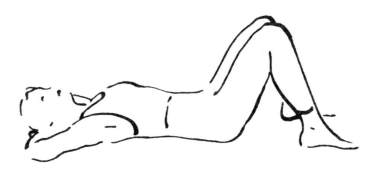

Lie on your back, hands by your sides, knees bent, feet flat on floor hip width apart. Pull in and flatten your tummy (abdominals) as you tilt the pelvis upwards and press lower back to the floor. There should be no 'space' between the lower back and floor as you adopt this position. Hold for 3 counts and release. Repeat 6 times.

9. ABDOMINAL CURL
To strengthen and tone abdominals.

Lie on your back, both knees bent, feet hip width apart and lower back pressed to the floor. With your hands behind your head, elbows out wide, ease head back into hands to support its weight. Now pull in and flatten tummy (abdominals) as you slowly lift head and shoulders 1 or 2 inches above the floor, then slowly lower. Keep head and neck in line with the spine. Chin up, head back and 'lift' leading with the chest. Exhale as you lift, inhale as you lower. Repeat 5–10 times.

10. ABDOMINAL OBLIQUE REACH
To strengthen and tone waist.

This is performed as above but release right hand from behind head (left hand supporting weight of head). Keep right arm close to right side of body and face the ceiling. Gently reach right fingers towards right ankle and move directly to the side. Squeeze into right side of waist and release. For added resistance raise shoulders slightly. Repeat.

11. KNEE HUG
To release tension in abdominals and ease out lower back.

Lie on floor, knees bent (as in previous exercise). Slowly bring your knees into chest. Holding underneath the knee joints pull knees towards chest. The lower back and chest are relaxed to the floor. Hold 10 seconds.

12. ABDOMINAL STRETCH
To stretch abdominals, rib cage, spine, shoulders, arms and feet.

Lie on floor, knees bent. Slowly raise arms above head as you slide feet away to extend legs. Now point toes and fingers in opposite directions. To stop lower back from arching, slightly bend knees as you lengthen the whole body. Breathe deeply and gently increase the stretch as you exhale.

13. COMPLETE RELAXATION

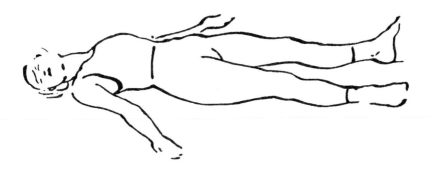

From the abdominal stretch above, slowly bring your hands down by your sides, palms facing ceiling. Let your feet relax outwards, roll your head to one side, close eyes and relax. Let the whole body become heavy and 'melt' into floor. With deep steady breathing try to empty your mind and let any thoughts drift away. Relax in this position for as long as you wish.

Walking Masterclass – The Walk Slim Maintenance Plan

When you started this plan your initial motivation was to lose weight and get fit. Now, after 30 days you should be well on your way to achieving the weight loss you desire and you will be looking ahead to maintaining the weight loss forever. You've already done the hard work.

So how do you keep it up?

When you started out, we set the goals. From now on the goals are going to be set by you. Providing you follow the Walk Slim Diet and walk aerobically for 30 minutes, four times a week – the rest is up to you. As long as you are performing this minimum amount of exercise, you will be doing sufficient to maintain aerobic fitness and you will be able to maintain your weight loss

As you will have already discovered, walking is about much

more than weight loss and fitness. It's about self-esteem, self-confidence, relaxation, easing away stress. In the end you walk because you want to walk; it makes you feel good; it's fun.

If you keep it up, after three months you will be a master-walker. Nothing will stop you walking at every opportunity you can find. Walking will become an important part of your weekly routine and you will want to keep it up for a lifetime.

PART TWO

2

FIT KIDS
Fitness for All the Family

*Train up a child in the way he should go: and when he is
old, he will not depart from it.*

PROVERBS 22, 6

We have all seen the cartoons highlighting our inactivity and telling us that most of us are couch potatoes. Well, take a look again – for increasing numbers of our children are also couch potatoes. And it's official.

A study of nearly 24,000 youngsters, whose ages ranged from 12 to 16, carried out by the Schools Health Education Unit at Exeter University in England, found the following disturbing truth: nearly half the girls and one-third of the boys take less exercise than the equivalent of one 10-minute brisk walk a week.

And a two-year fitness survey by education chiefs in Peterborough, Cambridgeshire, involving 800 youngsters from seven junior schools, discovered that many children were so out of condition that they were unable to take part in playground games such as skipping, running and hopscotch. One comment made was that: 'Children have more facilities to play indoors. They don't go out as often as they should.'

And a recent study in the USA by the Department of Health and Human Services found that 40 per cent of children between the age of 5 and 8 were shown to exhibit at least one of the following heart disease risk factors: obesity, hypertension and high blood cholesterol, and the reason given was inactivity and a sedentary lifestyle.

Dr Kenneth Cooper, author of *Aerobics*, says that 'kids are heavier and less fit aerobically now than 15 years ago' and this is due to 'sedentary living and poor nutrition'.

In the UK and the USA, with up to 90 per cent of adults failing to exercise sufficiently to benefit long-term health, it seems that children are following in their parents' footsteps. With the increasing use of the motor car to ferry children around; with some children watching up to 25 hours of television each week; and with video and computer games taking the place of sports and fitness activities, is it any wonder that increasing numbers of children are overweight and unfit?

Many people, of course, are hoping that schools will keep children active, but unfortunately school physical education programmes are failing to do the job. Tight school budgets and lack of playing fields and sports facilities all contribute to the problem, and even where schools have good sports facilities, there is often a focus on competitive team games rather than individual activities which promote long-term health and fitness.

Emphasis on skills needed to play soccer, rugby, netball and cricket takes precedence over cardiovascular endurance, suppleness, strength, flexibility and body weight maintenance – the requirements for a fit and healthy body. We teach children the 3 Rs and how to compete, but we don't teach them the simple skill of regular fitness walking: the easiest and cheapest way for children of all ages to get fit and keep fit for life.

With increasing evidence that physical inactivity in children increases the risk of heart disease, and with schools increasingly unable to provide suitable activities which foster long-term fitness and health, the main force behind motivating children must come from parents.

In 1987, The National Child Youth Fitness Study in the USA revealed that sedentary parents tend to have sedentary children and active parents tend to have active children. And a recent University of Pittsburgh study found that overweight children have greater long-term success controlling their weight if they are involved in a family-based exercise and diet programme. So the moral is that your children are more likely to keep fit and watch their weight if you do. And it's never too late for them to start.

Dr Neil Armstrong in charge of Exeter University's Physical Education Research Centre said: 'You are never going to persuade all children to do aerobics, but 80 per cent can do more walking.' And Arnold Schwarzenegger, the film star, who is chairman of the President's Council on Physical Fitness and Sports in the USA, offers the following advice: 'Parents must make fitness a family affair. How can Mom and Dad help? They can participate in exercise activities with their children. They can turn off the TV and encourage all family members to get out into the yard or on the street for a brisk walk.'

How Active is Your Child?

The minimum recommendation in Britain for children's fitness is that they should exercise vigorously (get out of breath) for at least 15 minutes, 3 to 5 times a week. In the USA the American Academy of Pediatrics and the American College of Sports Medicine both recommend that children should engage in 20 to 30 minutes of vigorous exercise each day. So how active is your child? Does your child:

- sit in front of the TV or computer screen for hours on end?
- get out of breath walking up stairs?
- prefer to have a lift in the car rather than walk short distances?
- live on a high-fat diet?
- seem to be putting on excess weight?
- lack motivation to exercise regularly?
- get bored easily?

If this is what your child is like then you have a problem, because your child is on a fast track to becoming an unhealthy adult. According to research conducted by the Institute for Aerobics Research in Dallas, USA, 'at least 30 to 35 per cent of school-age children are at risk for heart or circulatory disease and for premature death as adults'. Dr Kenneth Cooper, of the Aerobics Institute, advises: 'Starting a lifetime aerobic exercise programme now will greatly reduce your child's risk of dying from sedentary living as an adult.'

Since walking is the easiest way for children to exercise aerobically, then you should get your children active as soon as possible – and get them walking.

Why Your Child Should Walk

'Walking is far better for children than running,' says Dr Lyle Micheli, director of Sports Medicine at The Children's Hospital in Boston. 'Because of its low impact, it prevents the injured tissue and joint injuries we've seen in children who exert two-and-a-half to five times their body weight while running.'

Walking works because it is a low-impact, low-stress activity and is the safest aerobic exercise for kids, since their feet strike the ground with only 1–1.5 times their body weight. Walking is a moderate exercise, so the strength of kids' legs and cardiovascular endurance improves gradually without strain or injury.

Children who walk regularly develop in much the same way as adults – they increase their stamina, strength and flexibility. Although aerobic capacity increases regardless of training as a child grows, children who walk regularly will achieve greater aerobic capacity than sedentary kids. And that's not all that walking will do for your kids:

WALKING...
- helps develop good posture
- firms and tones muscles, improving body shape
- burns stored body fat and helps weight loss
- promotes strong bone growth, reducing the risk of osteo-porosis in later life
- reduces the risk of heart disease and back pain
- makes kids physically and mentally more alert

- fosters independence and self-reliance
- encourages kids to think for themselves
- increases confidence, self-esteem and self-image

Walking is a non-competitive activity, doesn't require any special equipment and can be done equally well by boys and girls. Regular walking can enhance a child's reading, writing and other skills, and their increased aerobic fitness will help them cope with the pressures of school and examinations.

Walking is one activity that your kids can keep up for a lifetime.

The Family Walk

Walk Together/Talk Together

It's fun, it's free and it's the easiest way for all the family to get fit together. Escape from the stresses and strains of modern indoor life – the television, the telephone, the computer, the feeling of living on top of each other – and get outside in the open air and walk together.

'Walking is an excellent exercise, available to everybody. I encourage regular family walks – at least a half an hour a day. It's a good way to spend time with your kids and a healthy habit,' says Dr Leo Galland, an international nutrition expert.

In our modern urban society, families are spending less time together. Jobs often force parents into long hours commuting; children are in school much of the day; parents and children are involved in separate activities in the evening. As a result, meals are eaten separately and there is little interaction and communication between family members.

Even exercise can get in the way of family interaction. With dad going for a game of squash and mum off to an aerobics class, children's fitness is often ignored, with parents thinking that the school will look after it. And as we have already seen, this is far from the truth.

The answer to the problem is for families to find ways of being together – to share common experiences and co-operate with each other. Often it's difficult to find an activity which all the family can do together. Not everyone has the same skills and motivation to play ball games or take part in sports activities, but the one activity that everyone can take part in is a family walk.

Walking is the only activity where everyone starts out on an equal footing! After all, we all walk, even our grandparents, so it's just a matter of getting the family together and deciding to walk regularly.

Walking is one of the few physical activities that lets you concentrate as much on each other as on the exercise. Not only will walking build a strong healthy body but it will also build a strong, healthy family bond.

Whether your goal is to get the family talking together or to get them active, the key is to make it fun. Kids often have a short attention span so it's essential to vary your walks so that they don't get bored and want to give up. When it comes to fitness, boredom is one of the biggest excuses for people giving up. So you must make it fun. The following are fun ways in which you can keep your children's interest:

- Tell your kids ahead of time so that they can look forward to a special outing. Anticipation keeps kids' attention and they will be more motivated to walk when the time arrives.

- Vary the route as much as possible. Alternate walks in the local neighbourhood with walks to the park, and trips to the countryside or seaside at weekends when you have more time.

- Nature walks, both in town and countryside, can provide an opportuniy for kids to look, find and learn more about the world around them. Spotting birds and identifying flowers and trees are all ways to heighten children's awareness and appreciation of their environment. On their walks they can learn more about the weather, history, geography, vegetation, science and animals.

- Walk to a surprise destination – a zoo or a playground, or visit a castle or museum. For a treat, let your kids decide where they would like to walk. Let them take a friend with them.

- Bridge the generation gap – take grandma and grandad. A family walk provides time and relaxation for everyone to get together and share experiences.

Walking is an activity that can be enjoyed every day and kids should be encouraged to walk most days. Any amount of walking, however short, is healthy and is better than no exercise, but too much too soon can result in sore muscles and a loss of enthusiasm.

Kids should build up their walking gradually, increasing the speed and length a little at a time. At first, it is more important to walk regularly than to try and walk too far. Slower, long walks can be alternated with faster, short walks, giving low and high intensity workouts. Kids, like adults, should warm-up before walking briskly. The best warm-up is slow walking.

Walk with your family – you'll rediscover your feet and you'll rediscover each other. The family that walks together talks together.

Safe Walking

Walking together as a family is an ideal opportunity for teaching children road safety and to reinforce safety codes promoted by education authorities. The following safety code was provided by Ray Foan, Accident Risk Reduction Programme Manager for West Berkshire Priority Care Service – NHS Trust.

During your family walks talk about road safety to your children and impress upon them the need to do the following:

USING THE PAVEMENT
- walk on the nearside of the pavement away from the road edge
- cross the road at traffic lights or at a recognised crossing point

- look both ways twice before stepping out into the road and make sure there is time to cross without hurrying
- watch out for other oncoming pedestrians who may not give way to you, forcing you to step off the pavement onto the road
- learn to recognise the sounds of other road users – cars, buses, trucks, cyclists and motor cyclists
- at all times follow the basic highway code: STOP, LOOK and LISTEN

USING AN UNPAVED ROAD
- walk facing oncoming traffic, so you can see them and they can see you
- day or night, wear bright clothes or fluorescent strips so you can be seen by other road users
- use your senses, sight, sound and smell – if in doubt stop

We hope that we have persuaded you that walking is the easiest and safest exercise for your kids and the best way to keep healthy as a family.

3

STEP OUT TO A LONGER LIFE
Fitness for the Over 50s

Stay young – stay active
CICERO: 44BC

A walk is one of the secrets for dodging old age
RALPH WALDO EMERSON

There is a saying in China that 'old age is inevitable, but there is no excuse for senility'. The ageing process varies from person to person, and although it is inevitable, experts now agree that most people could look younger, be fitter, feel more vital and live longer if they exercised regularly throughout their lives.

Huber Warner, PhD of the National Institute on Ageing in the USA, is 55 and says: 'People should be concerned about ageing from the earliest stages of their lives. The problems of ageing are cumulative, and the sooner you start correcting them, the better off you are in the long run.'

It's never too late to start.

As you get older the effects of sedentary living and a passive lifestyle start to catch up with you – weak muscles, reduced stamina and suppleness, reduction in aerobic capacity and proneness to disease. By walking regularly and following the additional exercises in the wholebody fitness section of the book, you can increase your aerobic capacity, strength, stamina and suppleness even into the last decades of your life.

Walk Longer – Live Longer

Take a two-mile walk every morning before breakfast
HARRY TRUMAN
(advice on how to live to be 80, on his 80th birthday)

They say that 'old age puts more wrinkles on our minds than on our faces'. You are as old as you feel. A 50-year-old who feels 40 is 40 – a 40-year-old who feels 50 is 50. A bored 40-year-old is the same as a bored 50-year-old. In the fight against ageing, mental fitness is as important as physical fitness.

Mental fitness gets you up and going; mental fitness gives you a new attitude, a new outlook to life; mental fitness gives you the drive and energy to make plans for a healthy future.

Many people drift into old age as though it's inevitable. They make financial plans for their middle age and retirement but they don't give the same consideration to a physical plan in order to enjoy these years to the full. They drift into their middle and later years sitting around waiting for a heart attack, when what they should be doing is following an exercise and diet plan to help them enjoy life to the full.

It's not the passing years that's a problem – it's a passive lifestyle. By their 50s more than 40 per cent of males and 80 per cent of females are sedentary – they spend too much time sitting.

To give you some idea just how a passive lifestyle can damage your health, a report in a US magazine, *Prevention*, in February 1991, estimated that 22,000 people in New York alone might die during the year 'clinging to their armchairs'.

A sedentary lifestyle is considered so bad for you that the American Heart Association now lists it as a major 'risk factor' on a par with high blood cholesterol, high blood pressure and cigarette smoking. The Center for Disease Control in Atlanta, USA, found that the least active people were almost twice as likely to have heart disease as the most active.

There are many aspects of your life over which you have no control – but you do have control over your exercise and diet. Getting started now and making small changes to your lifestyle will help you regain aerobic capacity, stamina, strength and flexibility. And the easiest way to do this is to walk regularly and follow *The Walk Slim Diet*.

Dr Ralph Paffenberger of Stanford University in the USA, in *The College Alumni Study* found that people who walked regularly were significantly less likely to suffer or die from a heart attack than their less active colleagues, and men who walked 9 or more miles a week had a 21 per cent lower mortality rate than those who walked 3 miles or less. He also found that the benefits tended to increase with age.

And it's not just cardiovascular health that improves: walking helps with back pain, arthritis, osteoporosis, varicose veins, reducing cholesterol, and other medical problems where inactivity is a factor.

By walking regularly you cut your rate of physical decline by half. 'Use it or lose it' is the adage. If you don't exercise, muscles deteriorate, your aerobic capacity deteriorates and you have less stamina, strength and flexibility. Life becomes a strain and you have less energy and vitality to get you through the day.

Aerobic capacity (the ability of the cardiovascular system to deliver oxygen to working muscles) declines slightly every year after the age of 30. After 30, your maximum heart rate declines and your lungs and blood vessels become less elastic. Because your heart and lungs supply less oxygen to your tissues, your vitality diminishes each year and you tire more easily.

What you need is an oxygen bath! This is what walking will do for you:

AEROBIC ENDURANCE
- improves cardiovascular fitness
- improves respiratory capacity
- improves muscle endurance
- burns calories to help maintain optimal body weight
- raises HDL, 'good' cholesterol
- reduces psychological stress
- guards against heart disease and other health problems

STRENGTH AND FLEXIBILITY

- delay loss of strength and muscle mass
- maintain muscle tone and joint range of motion
- assist balance and good posture
- slow bone shrinkage and weakening

Regular aerobic walking will make your heart stronger and fitter. It will give you a better figure and it will help shape and tone your body and keep off those unwanted pounds. And it will help you feel fitter mentally.

Aerobic walking improves fitness and slows ageing. 'By improving your physical fitness, you'll look and feel much younger than your calendar age,' says Dr Kenneth H. Cooper, author of *Aerobics*, and a firm advocate of the benefits of walking.

So if you want to have a healthy heart, strong muscles and flexible joints then walking will help you do this. Regular walking will add years to your life and life to your years.

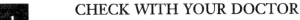

5 STEPS TO A LONGER LIFE

The best way to lengthen out our days is to walk steadily and with a purpose
CHARLES DICKENS

1   CHECK WITH YOUR DOCTOR

If you have been inactive for some time, or have a diagnosed medical problem which may inhibit you taking exercise, or are unsure about your current state of health, then check with your doctor first. Show him this book and seek his advice before starting out with a vigorous walking programme.

2   BUILD SLOWLY

Even if you are reasonably fit and active, you will still need to start slowly and ease yourself gently into a regular walking programme. Doctors agree that there are no risks with regular exercise as long as you warm-up first and start gently.

So put on a comfortable pair of walking shoes and do the warm-up exercises in Part 1. Then start out with a 10-minute walk and gradually increase your walk to 20 minutes over two weeks. At this point you are not concerned with distance, speed or target heart rates – simply walking and building a regular habit.

As you increase your stride and get into a good rhythm, walk at a speed that feels comfortable. Listen to your body – it's the best judge of how you feel. When you've finished your walk you should feel relaxed and refreshed. If you feel tired, you are going too fast. Conversational walking pace is a good guide: you should be able to hold a conversation without getting out of breath.

Since some of you are likely to be using muscles that you haven't used for years, you can expect some soreness as part of the natural process of strengthening muscles, but too much is unhealthy. If you experience this, then give yourself a few days rest before walking again.

After two weeks you should be able to walk for 20 minutes comfortably without straining yourself, but for those of you who still find this difficult, then continue walking for as many weeks as you need before moving on to the more vigorous walking workouts in Chapter 1.

WATCH YOUR WEIGHT

You will feel better and have more stamina and energy if you attain your ideal body weight. One of the best ways to lose weight is regular aerobic walking. For every 30 minutes walking you lose around 200 calories on average, and if you combine this with *The Walk Slim Diet*, then you will burn off extra calories and easily be able to get back to and maintain your correct weight.

The average woman in her 20s has about 27 per cent body fat. But by the time she's 50 that has increased to a whopping 42 per cent! For men, 18 per cent can grow to 30–35 per cent by the age of 50. As muscle is replaced with fat and metabolic rate tends to slow down with increasing age, then it is even more important to exercise and eat healthily.

WALK WITH OTHERS

4

The historian, G. M. Trevelyan, who was a great walker, said: 'Walking is a land of many paths and no paths, where everyone goes his own way and is right.' Some people will want to walk alone; like Trevelyan they find a sense of independence in the great outdoors. But many people will prefer company, and walking with a friend, spouse or the family is an excellent way to get motivated and build a habit to last a lifetime.

You may want to organise your own walking club in the area where you live, or at work. Some people form walking clubs to walk during their lunch hour or after work.

KEEP IT UP

5

At least 25 per cent of people who start exercise programmes give up in the first week. So don't exercise too hard and then give up through boredom or injury. Take it slowly, keep motivated and keep walking. You will soon start to see results, and as you discover for yourself how easy it is to walk regularly, you will find that you want to get out as often as possible and knock up all those aerobic miles.

Don't be disheartened if there are days when you don't want to walk, when your enthusiasm fails you. Another day will come around and you will be bursting to get outside in the open air and clock up more miles. As your aerobic fitness increases, the feeling of increased stamina, energy and vitality will be enough to get you out and about.

Special Considerations

It has been estimated that 50 per cent of the decline in biological functions between the ages of 30 and 70 is due to disuse. The so-called 'diseases of civilisation' could be more accurately called diseases of physical inactivity. The following conditions can all be relieved by walking regularly, but this advice is not a substitute for expert medical advice. If you suffer from one of these conditions you should consult your doctor before starting a walking programme.

Can walking help my back pain?

Four out of five people experience back pain at some time in their lives. Back pain accounts for 6.5 per cent of all visits to the doctor, and it causes the loss of 67 million working days a year in Britain at a cost of £3 billion.

Years of inactivity – too much time spent sitting and too little time spent exercising – causes back problems due to bad posture which weakens back muscles. Back pain can be alleviated by building strength and flexibility in the muscles that support your spine, particularly the hamstrings, quadriceps, abdominals, lower back and laterals.

'Taking a walk regularly is one of the best things you can do for your back,' says Dr John Regan, a surgeon at the Texas Back Institute. 'It promotes muscular development and increases circulation.'

Walking, which is a low-stress, low-impact activity, will help strengthen your back and help tone and stretch your back muscles. And regular walking promotes weight control and good posture and helps reduce muscle tension – key factors in maintaining a healthy back. Carrying around excess weight strains back muscles, creates bad posture and increases compression of the spinal discs. Remember, always warm up before walking and cool down after your walking session.

If you have a back problem, you may actually feel better walking than sitting. According to Swedish back expert Dr Alf Nachemson, walking puts less strain on the spine than does unsupported sitting. Walking strengthens the muscles in the pelvis and lower back and the forward movement of the body reduces the force of gravity on your back.

To develop whole body fitness and full mobility in the back, you should follow the simple stretching and strengthening exercises in The Whole-Body Workout.

Can walking help my arthritis?

Doctors used to advise arthritic patients against exercising but it is now more common for doctors to prescribe exercise. Walking helps to strengthen the muscles around joints, relieves pain when muscles rub together and can prevent joint inflammation.

It's important to take it gently, rest frequently and don't walk through pain. Warm-up thoroughly first, walk only as far as feels comfortable and increase the length of your walk gradually. Discuss the problem with your doctor. You may need to do some additional strengthening and stretching exercises of the type shown in The Whole-Body Workout.

Because arthritis often causes depression leading to lethargy and inactivity, walking helps because it is a natural mood elevator, releasing beta-endorphins (relaxation hormones) in the brain which increase your sense of well being.

Can walking help prevent osteoporosis?

Osteoporosis (thinning of the bones) is a condition that gradually robs bones of their strength, leaving them so brittle that an action as simple as tying a shoelace can result in a fracture.

As we age, the mineral content of our bones decreases,

their texture becomes thinner and there is a gradual decrease in skeletal strength. Osteoporosis affects many post-menopausal women due to the decrease of the hormone oestrogen and it affects women more than men – 1 in 40 men but 1 in 4 women suffer from this condition.

The following are risk factors that can all be modified:

- being sedentary
- inadequate calcium intake
- cigarette smoking
- being underweight
- a deficiency of vitamin D

Bones are similar to muscles in that they shrink from inactivity and benefit from exercise. Walking, as a weight-bearing exercise, can help your bones maintain and also gain strength and density. The force of gravity, and the physical act of walking, causes your muscles to pull on your bones which stimulates the bone to take in more strengthening calcium.

Calcium and exercise are the main keys in the prevention of osteoporosis. A good calcium diet nourishes and maintains bones and regular exercise helps to maintain a strong skeleton. Sources of calcium are milk and milk products, green, leafy vegetables, citrus fruits and shellfish.

Some experts think that a reduction in regular physical activity is the major reason for a rise in osteoporosis in the past 30 years. William Evans, PhD, of Tufts University in the USA, has studied the effects of walking for the treatment of osteoporosis and he says: 'From what we see, exercise may be one of the best ways to stop or prevent age-related bone loss.'

Can walking help control diabetes?

A combination of regular aerobic walking, *The Walk Slim Diet* and weight loss will make it easier for people with adult-onset diabetes to control their condition. Walking increases the body's sensitivity to insulin and increases the uptake of blood sugar (glucose) by the muscles.

And walking can actually reduce your chance of developing diabetes. That's the conclusion of a study involving 122,000 American nurses (*The Lancet*, September 1991). One group of nurses exercised regularly – brisk walking, jogging, cycling, etc. The other group took no exercise and twice as many of them developed diabetes.

PART THREE

4

STRESSBUSTER
Take Control of your Life

To all who feel overwhelmed and work weary, the exhilarating exercise of walking offers both a stimulus and a sedative

ROBERT LOUIS STEVENSON

From the moment we rise in the morning to the moment we go to bed life grinds us down. Physically, the force of gravity grinds us down – at the end of the day we are up to three-quarters of an inch shorter due to the compression of cartilages in our spine. And mentally, we all experience the increasing pace and pressure of life which can leave us feeling tense, tired and listless. In simple words – we feel stressed.

Ninety million working days are lost in the UK each year through undue stress in the workplace – that's 30 times more than time lost through strikes – and the total cost to industry has been estimated at £7.5 billion a year. Doctors estimate that 75 to 90 per cent of people visiting them suffer from stress-related problems.

But what is stress?

Stress is the disease of the 20th century. We all suffer from it, but it's not so much the amount of stress in our lives which is the problem, but our ability to cope with it.

We feel stressed when everything simply gets too much for us – we feel tense, anxious or depressed. The increasing pace of life, social change, work, financial worries, divorce, retirement and bereavement all contribute to stress. Even some types of exercise can be stressful. With the average woman now working up to 15 hours a week longer than a man, juggling the demands of a home, children and job, is it any wonder that in the end the mind and body cannot take any more.

Although there are many causes of stress, one of the major causes is physical inactivity. Sitting for much of the day in one form of chair or another – domestic chairs, office chairs, cars, buses, trains and taxies – we drag our sedentary, over-stimulated, over-stressed bodies back home in the evening where many of us then spend another three hours a night sitting in chairs watching television.

A recent report by the British Heart Foundation said that lack of exercise is almost as bad for the heart as smoking 20 cigarettes a day, having high blood pressure or high levels of cholesterol. **And one of its main recommendations was for people to walk briskly.**

In the USA the problem of physical inactivity is now so serious that the American Heart Association recently changed the status of physical inactivity from a 'contributory factor' for heart, blood vessel diseases and stroke to a 'risk factor'. This puts a sedentary lifestyle on a par with high blood cholesterol, high blood pressure and cigarette smoking.

Throughout the Western world a sedentary lifestyle (inactivity) is now recognised as a major cause of ill health. Inactivity slows down your metabolism. You feel tired and lethargic. By the evening all you want to do is slump in a chair and go to sleep.

Inactivity breeds inactivity and it breeds tension: your muscles are wound up, your mind is wound up, you have a stiff neck and a stiff back, and to make matters worse your body burns less calories so you put on weight. In time, your muscles and bones begin to atrophy so you get old before your time.

To cope with stress and inactivity you need to take control of your life. When you feel stressed, you are out of control – circumstances are controlling you. Research from the US shows that the feeling of having no control is the major source of stress for women. Although there may be many circumstances that you cannot change, one area of your life that you can change is your level of activity.

Normally, when the body cries out for a break from tension and stress there are two types of response. One is to ply the body with coffee, snacks, alcohol or cigarettes – which only makes matters worse; the other is to relax, become more active and ease away the stress naturally. And the easiest way to do this is to walk.

The simple pleasure of getting out of the house or the office and using your legs gives you the feeling of being in control. Walking is more effective than a gin and tonic and is less demanding than jogging or a game of squash. Walking gets you away from the world of competitive work and competitive sport, and gives you the peace and quiet to relax naturally. Walking is the natural way to cope with stress.

Walking – A Natural Therapy

Walking is a delectable madness, very good for sanity
COLIN FLETCHER

Walking helps you take control of your life and put some fun back in it. You start saying no to the things that get you down and you get out on the road and walk and smile at the world. Your body is not built for sitting around all day; it's built for movement, especially walking. Your body functions best when it's walking rhythmically at 3.5–4 miles per hour.

A main theme of this book has been the idea of rhythm and its power to heal. The healing power of rhythm unlocks destructive emotions and creates harmony out of disorder. When you walk you rediscover a sense of rhythm – your sense of rhythm, a rhythm which moves through every fibre of your body energising you.

Walking recharges your physical and mental batteries; a good walk refreshes your body and mind, and is the best antidote to tension. Even a short, aerobic walk can drain away tensions before they turn into headaches, back aches, high blood pressure and insomnia. Aerobic walking is a powerful therapeutic tool:

- aerobic walking can reduce tension, anxiety and mood swings

- aerobic walking can reduce headaches, back aches and muscle tension
- aerobic walking can reduce high blood pressure
- aerobic walking can reduce depression
- aerobic walking can reduce emotional fatigue
- aerobic walking can reduce boredom
- aerobic walking can reduce insomnia

And aerobic walking will improve or increase your:

- self-confidence
- self-image
- feelings of independence
- optimism
- relaxation
- creative energy
- immune system
- control over your life

Walking uses up stress hormones which otherwise stay in the blood, keeping us tense. Aerobic walking works by decreasing the stress hormones (epinephrine and norepinephrine) and increasing relaxation hormones in the brain (beta-endorphins). These hormones help to elevate your mood and give you a sense of well being – a sort of 'walker's high'.

You will feel the tranquillising effect of walking not just in your mind, but in your body due to the improved oxygen supply and the reduction of carbon dioxide in the blood. Increased oxygen supply improves memory, thinking ability and concentration. Away from pressure and stress, you give your mind a holiday – a mini-vacation.

It is the continuous, vigorous, rhythmic motion of aerobic walking which breaks down the pattern of stress and puts you in a new frame of mind. No other game, sport or activity can give you the benefits that aerobic walking can give you. Away from the television, telephone and nagging domestic and professional worries, your problems become a thing of the past.

Got a Problem? Walk It Off

A turn or two I'll walk to still my beating mind.
SHAKESPEARE, *The Tempest*

Have you ever had a nagging problem which seemed insoluble? A difficult boss at work? Financial worries? A feeling that everything was getting just too much for you?

Well, instead of reaching for the aspirin bottle, get outside in the fresh air and try walking. The rhythmic action of walking will help you work out your problems. Dr George Sheehan, the American walker who recommends his patients to walk, has said, 'Never trust an idea lying down.' The Latin phrase 'ambulando solvitur' sums it up – walking is good for problem solving.

The gentle rhythmic swing of the arms back and forth has a meditational effect on the mind similar to transcendental and Zen meditation. Aerobic walking restores to your mind a sense of balance, which counteracts the harmful effects of cumulative stress. A walk is a refreshing break; a time you make for yourself; a time to just let go and let your problems dissolve away.

During the normal workday, your mind sets the pace and drives you on. But it is the mind, the 'conscious mind' that is much of the problem when it comes to tension, anxiety, depression – stress. We get stuck in its repetitive patterns: we get uptight at times over seemingly nothing; we get upset when things don't go our way; and even serious problems get out of hand and seem to be insoluble. We need to walk.

Walking puts life in perspective. It allows you to take a broad view about what's bothering you. It's a dynamic process. It replaces the tense, repetitive patterns of the conscious mind with the healing repetitive motion of brisk, aerobic exercise.

Walking energises you and wakes you up to the realisation of who you really are. It gives you the mental and physical stamina to cope with life.

In George Meredith's novel *The Egoist*, Miss Middleton

asked of Mr Whitford, 'Have you walked far today?' His reply was 'Nine and a half hours . . . I had to walk off my temper.'

You don't have to walk for nine and a half hours to feel the benefits of regular aerobic walking and get away from stress. A 10-minute walk will boost your spirits and make you feel more energetic than eating a bar of chocolate. Ten minutes is enough and you can do it at any time of the day.

Coping with a Stressful Day

An early morning walk is a blessing for the whole day
THOREAU

Henry David Thoreau was one of the great American walkers along with his friend, the writer Ralph Waldo Emerson. Emerson said: 'I believe that in our good days, a well-ordered mind has a new thought awaiting it each morning.' Both men believed in the magic and power of early morning walks.

And Dorothy Wordsworth in her *Journals* describes how her brother 'walks out every morning'. William Wordsworth's lifelong habit was to compose his poetry while walking out of doors in the Lake District.

Get out and walk before your normal day begins. Walk aerobically for at least 10 minutes, 20–30 if you can spare the time. As you feel the rhythm and movement through your feet and legs and as oxygen surges through your bloodstream, your body gears up for the day ahead and gives you the energy and stamina to cope.

Between 3 a.m. and 5 a.m. most people's hormone levels are depressed, and their heart rate and body temperature are down. As they rise and start their day, their bodies are sluggish and half awake – it takes until lunchtime to get warmed up and into the day. An early morning walkout gets you going, warms up your body and your mind, and gives you a physical and psychological edge on the day.

People often ask, 'But where am I going to find the time?' Put the alarm on 30 minutes earlier. An early morning walk will do you far more good than the extra sleep or simply lying in bed awake, unable to rouse yourself. And it's far more effective than a cup of coffee.

But remember to warm up thoroughly. Build up your pace over 4 or 5 minutes and then do your warm-up stretches before you stride out into a brisk walk.

Like Emerson, you will find that your mind is filled with positive thoughts that can help you through the day.

Afternoon Walks

The novelist Charles Dickens who walked every afternoon said: 'If I could not walk far and fast I think I would just explode and perish.' Jane Austen in her novel, *Northanger Abbey*, has one of her characters say: 'The afternoon was made for walking.'

Although your body reaches its peak in the afternoon, afternoons can also be peak anxiety time. So get out of the house or the office and walk away tension and anxiety before they have time to cause any damage. Instead of sitting around at lunchtime, take a brisk walk for 20–30 minutes and eat a nourishing Walk Slim lunch.

If you are pressed for time, try taking a brisk 10-minute walk instead of a coffee break. Robert E. Thayer, PhD of California State University in the USA, has done extensive research on the psychological benefits of walking and is the originator of the brisk 10-minute walk concept for stress reduction.

If you live near work then try walking home. If you use a bus or train then either walk a few stops before getting on, or get off a few stops earlier and walk the rest of the way home.

Evening Walks

The 16th-century philosopher Erasmus counselled his disciples: 'Before supper walk a little; after supper do the same.' When it comes to draining off the muscular tension that has built up during the day, walking is the world's most efficient tranquilliser.

The evening is a time for 'walking meditation'; a time to reflect on the day past; and a time to look forward to the day ahead. No matter what the day has thrown at us, an evening walk is the best antidote to stress.

Getting outside in the open air allows us to find a focus and put the day into perspective. Walking activates our sense of awe and wonder, and heightens our sensibility to nature. Walking gives us back our senses. We see, hear and smell the world anew.

The evening walk is a time to think pleasant thoughts: a time to take stock; a time to let go of fear, anger and doubt; a time to forgive others and ourselves. It is a time to let go of the negative feelings that stress imposes on us and let the positive effects of walking take over.

Positive walking is like positive thinking – it works. Walk tall and look the world right in the eye; make friends with the world and yourself. Lift your head higher, look ahead, feel the ground under you and put a sparkle and glow back into your life.

An evening walk will help you sleep. A short stroll prior to bedtime will decrease muscular tension and help you to relax. When the muscles are relaxed the brain goes to sleep more easily. Charles Dickens, himself a great walker, offers the following prescription: 'If you can't sleep, try walking.'

Body and Soul

According to the Roman philosopher, Seneca: 'The care of the soul is man's most important duty, because from the soul issue our thoughts, from the soul our words, from the soul our expressions and indeed our very gait.'

Vanda Scaravelli, a yoga teacher, describes in her book, *The Awakening of the Spine*, how we should walk: 'Carry your body, but please do not let your body carry you! Walking in the streets, one can see people heavily following their bodies. Their heads lean forwards, pulled by their necks, on their insecure legs, their feet scarcely touching the ground. It is evident that they are slaves to their bodies, following the whispering of their chattering minds.'

The way you walk says a lot about you to others; your body language says a lot about the state of your soul. A confident, fearless person who looks forward to the day ahead, walks tall and looks others and the world in the eye. An unsure, fearful person shuffles along, with eyes and mind unfocused, a prey to vague doubts, fears and uncertainty.

Walking allows us to get back in touch with our soul – our better self. Mind aerobics is as important as body aerobics. Mind aerobics is all about rediscovering yourself as the magnificent, positive creative person that you know you really are.

If, as some people believe, life is about 'rediscovering our inner child' or 'becoming again as a child', then walking is the easiest way to get back in touch with this child.

'On a day when I didn't have to wear a collar and tie I was a boy again,' said Alfred Wainwright, perhaps the best known walker in Britain. Wainwright knew all about the healing power of getting out on the open road with the sky above him and the wind in his hair.

The fastest way to still the mind, relax and get back in touch with your soul is to move the body. Walk, let go and surrender to your own natural rhythms – to the beat of your own heart, the wave of your own breath and the sound of your own inner music.

Walking is as natural as breathing. Chuang Tzu, the Chinese teacher, tells us that, 'The true man breathes with his heels.' The feet allow us to collect energy from the ground. The alternating rhythmic motion of the arms and legs is similar to the inhalation and exhalation of the lungs when we breathe. Breath control is one way of learning to meditate; another way is to walk.

In the early 18th century, Jean Jacques Rousseau, the prophet of the Romantic movement, had this to say about the meditative effects of walking: 'My body has to be on the move to set my mind going ... I can only meditate when I am walking. When I stop I cease to think; my mind only works with my legs.'

Try walking meditation (WM). Get into your stride, build up a walking rhythm and do some movement meditation or counting breaths. To relax and get back in touch with our souls we need to slow down. Stepping back from the relentless beliefs that drive us, we can step forward with our walking meditation into a new way of seeing and believing – a way which teaches us to be gentle with ourselves and others.

Thich Nhat Hanh writes in his *Guide to Walking Meditation*: 'Your steps are the most important thing ... they decide everything.' Walk mindfully and become aware of your movement through the air. Feel the spring of your heel and toes as they propel you forward; feel the pull of your muscles in your feet, legs and hips; and feel the rhythm of your arms and legs. Stay with these feelings and explore them.

Next focus your attention on your breathing. As you walk, try this Zen meditation: inhale and count mentally, 1,2,3,4,5,6,7,8,9,10, one count to each step, making the inhalation extend over the ten steps. Then exhale slowly through the nostrils, counting as before – 1,2,3,4,5,6,7,8,9,10 – one count to a step. Rest between breaths, then continue with the same rhythm of breath counting until you begin to feel tired. If counting to ten is too difficult for you, then start with five and build up gradually to ten.

Walking and Music

The healing power of music has been recognised throughout history. Music creates harmony out of discord and unlocks emotion, leaving us free to relax. Like walking, music draws away tension and anxiety and puts you back in touch with yourself.

Try taking a Walkman cassette player with you when you walk. You can either play a favourite piece of music or you can buy a specialist walking tape. There are several on the market and they are available in two types. One type matches heart beat with the beat of the music (say 120 beats per minute). The second type also matches heart beat and is more useful for beginners – it has a voice over on the music and works as a motivational aid. It has information on how to get started, slowly build up your pace, and how to walk to achieve maximum benefits. Specialist tapes are available for a wide range of musical tastes – pop, classical, swing, country and marches.

Remember – if you listen to music while you walk then look where you are going.

5

PUT YOUR HEART INTO WALKING

And now I see with eye serene
The very pulse of the machine
WILLIAM WORDSWORTH

The heart has been called the root of life. Its pulse first echoed in your mother's womb eight months before you were born, and its gentle rhythmic beat will be with you till the end of your days. For the heart never sleeps.

The heart is the most efficient pump in the world. Weighing 11 ounces, it is a blood-filled bag of muscle the size of a fist. Each day it pumps 5,000 gallons of blood around the body. It beats about 38 million times a year and in an average lifetime enough blood is circulated around the body to fill the Albert Hall.

Aristotle believed the heart to be an organ from which 'the motions of the body commence'. Certainly, the rhythm of the heart allows the brain to think, the lungs to breathe and the muscles to move. Each time your heart beats it pumps out oxygen-rich blood to feed your muscles and vital organs. It is then pumped back again to the heart and sent to the lungs to pick up more oxygen before it starts on its way again.

The heart is not only a part of our body but it is part of our language. We talk about someone being 'strong hearted' or 'weak hearted' and we urge people to 'be of good heart'. We express a sense of commitment when we do something 'with all our heart'. And we feel vital and alive when we are 'at the heart of things'.

Considering that the heart is so important to us, many of us fail to treat it with the respect it deserves. According to the World Health Organisation, worldwide cardiovascular diseases are 'public health enemy No. 1' taking 12 million lives each year. According to WHO estimates, a half of all these deaths are preventable, which means that 6 million lives could be saved annually.

The increase in cardiovascular diseases is linked in part to the ageing in populations but also to lifestyle and the main risk factors which influence heart health. It used to be said that a man is as old as his arteries, but it would be more accurate to say that a man is as young as his arteries. The way that we live our lives can affect our arteries and our heart. The statistics for coronary heart disease show that many of us urgently need to review our lifestyles – what we need is a 'change of heart'.

Heartbeat – The Rhythm of Health

My pulse, as yours, doth temperately
Keep time,
And makes as healthful music.
SHAKESPEARE, *Hamlet*

The main factors that put you at risk of coronary heart disease are:

1. high blood pressure
2. high levels of cholesterol in your blood
3. smoking
4. being overweight
5. sedentary lifestyle/lack of exercise
6. stress
7. type II diabetes

If you live a moderate lifestyle with none of the above risk factors then your chances of having a heart attack are relatively low. But the likelihood climbs as the number of risk factors increase. So you need to be aware of them, and you need to control them.

Risk factors are of two types – those that can be changed

and those that cannot. You cannot change your family history, your sex, your age or your racial grouping. But you can affect the above risks. High blood pressure and high blood cholesterol are both modifiable with exercise. And it's never too late to quit smoking. After giving up, the risks of a heart attack are reduced by 50 per cent after the first year and further risks are wiped out after five years.

We have already covered risk factors 4–6. Following *The Walk Slim Diet* and walking regularly will help you to keep these risk factors under control, keep your weight down and reduce stress in your life.

Overweight people are three times more likely to develop type II diabetes (risk factor 7), and diabetics are twice as likely to have a heart attack or stroke than those without the disease. So walk regularly to keep your weight normal and reduce the risk of diabetes.

There is now overwhelming medical evidence which shows that exercising moderately will cut your chances of having a heart attack by half. A two-year study at the Center for Disease Control in Atlanta, USA, found that the least active people were almost twice as likely to have heart disease as those who were most active. They also pointed out that while smoking, high blood pressure or high blood cholesterol may put a person at higher risk of heart disease, lack of exercise actually poses a greater threat.

And the famous Paffenberger study at Stanford University, USA, found that people who were sedentary had a 30 to 40 per cent greater risk of dying from coronary heart disease than those who exercised moderately.

Exercise is not a cure-all to prevent heart disease. The above risk factors all affect people in different ways, but if you want to keep fit and healthy and minimise your exposure to them, then you must take exercise to heart.

Why Walking is Good Medicine

I have two doctors, my left leg and my right
G. M. TREVELYAN

Your heart is a muscle that beats 24 hours a day for a lifetime but like all muscles it needs to be exercised so that it can pump more blood with each beat and save you energy. An unfit heart has more work to do. Then even simple tasks like walking to the shops or carrying the shopping can become quite tiring. If you exercise aerobically, then your muscles use oxygen more efficiently, your heart pumps more blood with each beat and it doesn't beat as fast. Aerobic exercise is vital for your heart.

Walking is the safest and most effective aerobic exercise for your heart because it is easy to begin a walking programme and easy to keep it up. Walking is an exercise that you can safely do for the rest of your life.

'Brisk walking is an excellent stamina-building exercise,' says the Health Education Authority in its Look After Your Heart campaign. 'Your heart will benefit most from the kind of activity that builds up stamina. The vigorous effort of moving your muscles rhythmically creates a greater demand for oxygen in the blood, and more work for the heart and lungs.'

The Health Education Authority goes on to say that: 'Regular activity of this kind improves the balance of fatty substances in the bloodstream, lowers the resting blood pressure level and strengthens the heart muscle.'

Recent research by the British exercise physiologist Dr Adrianne Hardman and her colleagues at Loughborough University found that fat levels in the blood after a fatty meal were lower in people who had taken a brisk walk the day before. Volunteers who took a two-hour brisk walk the day before a meal had 30 per cent less dietary fats in their blood than when they ate similar food after a day without exercise. And early research suggests similar benefits from brisk walking after a meal. It seems that brisk walking helps clear dangerous fats from the blood and cuts the risk of clogged arteries.

The team at Loughborough University had already studied the effects of exercise on cholesterol levels in the blood. Dr Hardman said: 'Regular walking can increase the levels of "good" cholesterol in the blood, reducing chances of a heart attack.' She claims that exercise is the best lifestyle change you can make to increase your HDLs (good cholesterol). And several studies in the USA have suggested that exercise like aerobic walking can increase HDL levels by as much as 10–20 per cent.

More than 40 scientific studies have now shown that moderate physical activity like brisk walking develops cardiovascular health and protects against heart disease.

WALKING	protects the heart by increasing its size and strength so it can pump more blood with fewer beats.
WALKING	increases the size and number of blood vessels for better and more efficient circulation.
WALKING	increases the amount of oxygen delivered to all tissues and cells.
WALKING	increases the efficiency of exercising muscles and blood circulation so that muscles and blood can process oxygen more easily.
WALKING	increases HDL (good) cholesterol which protects heart and blood vessels from fatty deposits.
WALKING	increases the ability to cope with stress which means you will be less prone to heart disease.

WALKING   decreases triglycerides (sugar fats) so they are not deposited on the lining of arteries.

WALKING   decreases blood pressure by improving elasticity of blood vessels – giving less resistance to the flow of blood and increasing oxygen flow to tissues and cells.

Experts are generally agreed that if you want to develop cardiovascular health and have a fit and healthy heart you should exercise and build up to:

FREQUENCY   3 times a week

INTENSITY   enough to get you slightly breathless, but still be able to carry on a conversation, or – an RPE (rate of perceived exertion) of 13 or 60 per cent to 80 per cent of your Target Heart Rate

TIME   20 to 30 minutes per session

Most exercise physiologists used to believe that it was necessary to exercise at 60 to 80 per cent of your maximum heart rate (50 to 60 per cent for the very unfit) to develop cardiovascular health, but recently the American College of Sports Medicine (which publishes exercise standards) suggested that exercising at a level of 50 per cent of maximum heart rate would give an aerobic workout and improve fitness and health.

Walking at a brisk 3.5 to 4 mph, a speed which will leave you slightly breathless but still able to carry on a conversation, will be sufficient for most people to achieve an aerobic workout and develop a healthy heart. For those who wish to measure target heart rate, then aim for 60 to 80 per cent of maximum heart rate (start with 50 per cent if you are unfit).

Alternatively, an RPE of 13 will give you a good cardiovascular workout.

It is as well to remember that one of the reasons why walking is so easy to do is that you can vary your walking intensity to suit your requirement. At low intensity you can walk for relaxation and fun; at medium intensity for weight loss; and at high intensity for cardiovascular conditioning.

The British Heart Foundation has recently released a short leaflet aptly named *Put Your Heart Into Walking*, and subtitled 'How to keep your heart healthy and happy by walking your way to fitness'. They suggest the following ways to make brisk walking part of your life:

- Build a walk into your journey to work. Get off the bus early, or park away from the office. Enjoy the challenge of longer walks in shorter times.
- Save the expense of driving to the shops – walk instead.
- Involve the family. Walking is good for children too, and it's a great way of exploring the countryside.
- Don't use a lift or escalator. Walking briskly up and down stairs is really good for the heart.

So the message is – keep your heart in shape. It is the most important prescription you will ever get. If you look after your heart your heart will look after you.

PART
FOUR

6

WALK SLIM DIET RECIPES

The following recipes are based on low-fat, high-fibre foods which allow you to eat healthily without counting calories. If you don't like one of the ingredients then substitute with a food that you do like from the same food group – substitute one vegetable for another or one type of fish or meat for another. The same applies if an ingredient is not available. For exmaple: Salmon, Apple and Cashew Nuts can equally be enjoyed as Tuna, Apple and Cashew Nuts.

The recipes are for two people but if you are cooking for the family or just for yourself then multiply or halve the quantities as necessary.

ITALIAN SALAD

radicchio or other salad leaves
4 thin slices salami
2 small pickled cucumbers
2 spring onions
1 large tomato
black olives
fresh basil leaves
½ lemon
freshly ground black pepper

Arrange the salad leaves on individual plates. Cut the salami, pickled cucumbers and spring onions into small pieces and the tomato into wedges and arrange on the salad leaves. Squeeze some lemon juice and grind some black pepper on to the salad. Garnish with the olives and fresh basil.

MEXICAN PRAWNS

2 large Iceberg lettuce leaves
75 g (3 oz) cooked prawns
stick of celery, cut into small pieces
2 spring onions, finely chopped
1 small green pepper, cut into small pieces
10 ml (2 tsp) lime juice
3 ml (½ tsp) chilli sauce
5 ml (1 tsp) reduced calorie mayonnaise
freshly ground black pepper
lime wedges

Put the lettuce leaves on serving dishes. Gently mix together the prawns, celery, spring onions and green pepper in a bowl. Mix together the lime juice, chilli sauce and reduced calorie mayonnaise and stir into the salad. Spoon the salad into the lettuce leaves. Add some freshly ground black pepper and garnish with the lime wedges.

PEPPER SALAD

1 red pepper
1 green pepper
50 g (2 oz) lean cooked ham
10 ml (2 tsp) reduced calorie mayonnaise
lemon juice
freshly ground black pepper

Cut each pepper lengthways into 4 pieces and remove the seeds. Grill under a medium heat for about 5 minutes on each side. Leave to cool then peel the skin from the peppers. Arrange 2 slices of red and 2 slices of green pepper like a star, on serving dishes, alternating the colours. Cut the ham into small pieces, mix with the mayonnaise then spoon on to the centre of the peppers. Squeeze some lemon juice and grind some black pepper on to the salad. Serve with toast triangles.

SPANISH SALAD

lettuce leaves
1 large tomato, thinly sliced
1 small red pepper, cut into circles
1 small onion, cut into thin slices
1 small tin tuna in brine, drained and flaked
6 asparagus spears, cooked
2 hard-boiled eggs, cut into quarters
lemon juice
freshly ground black pepper

Put the lettuce leaves on a serving dish with the slices of tomato, red pepper and onion on top. Arrange the asparagus, egg quarters and tuna on the salad. Squeeze some lemon juice and grind some black pepper over the salad.

SALADE NICOISE

1 tin tuna in brine, drained
4 anchovy fillets, soaked in milk to reduce saltiness

1 hard-boiled egg, quartered
8 green or black olives
crispy lettuce leaves, such as Cos
1 large tomato, cut into wedges
1 small green or red pepper, cut into small pieces
1 small onion, chopped
1 clove garlic, chopped
10 ml (2 tsp) lemon juice
5 ml (1 tsp) olive oil
freshly ground black pepper
lemon wedges

Combine all salad ingredients with the flaked tuna. Toss in the dressing of lemon juice and olive oil. Arrange the anchovy fillets, quarters of hard-boiled egg, olives and lemon wedges on the salad and grind some black pepper over the salad.

WALDORF SALAD

2 sticks celery
1 red apple
1 green apple
10 ml (2 tsp) chopped walnuts
1 small onion
15 ml (1 tbsp) low fat natural yogurt
lemon juice
freshly ground black pepper
watercress or other salad leaf

Cut the celery and apples into small pieces and grate the onion. Mix together with the yogurt and lemon juice. Arrange on a bed of watercress and garnish with the chopped walnuts. Grind some black pepper over the salad.

SALMON, APPLE AND CASHEW NUTS

150 g (6 oz) salmon, cooked and flaked
1 apple, cut into small pieces
15 ml (1 tbsp) cashew nuts, chopped

5 ml (1 tsp) lemon juice
10 ml (2 tsp) reduced calorie mayonnaise
freshly ground black pepper
lemon wedges
Iceberg lettuce leaves or other salad leaf

Mix the salmon, apple and nuts with the lemon juice and mayonnaise. Arrange on the lettuce leaves and grind some black pepper over the salad. Garnish with the lemon wedges.

TABBOULEH

125 g (5 oz) burghul (cracked wheat)
1 large tomato, cut into very small pieces
wedge of cucumber, cut into very small pieces
1 small onion, grated
25 g (1 oz) raisins
25 g (1 oz) pine nuts, chopped
15 ml (1 tbsp) chopped fresh mint
juice of 1 large lemon
5 ml (1 tsp) olive oil
freshly ground black pepper
watercress or other salad leaf
lemon wedges

Soak the burghul in cold water for 15 minutes, then rinse and drain, squeezing the water out. Put in a bowl with all the other ingredients, except the watercress and lemon wedges, and mix thoroughly. Arrange on a bed of watercress and garnish with lemon wedges.

TUSCAN SALAD

1 tin tuna in brine, drained
150 g (6 oz) cooked white haricot beans
1 small onion, preferably red, finely chopped
5 ml (1 tsp) olive oil
3 ml (½ tsp) red wine vinegar
5 ml (1 tsp) chopped fresh parsley

freshly ground black pepper
lemon wedges

Mix together the tuna, beans and half the chopped onion, taking care not to break the beans, and arrange on individual plates. Mix the olive oil, red wine vinegar and parsley, and dribble over the salad. Arrange the rest of the chopped onion on the salad and add freshly ground black pepper. Garnish with lemon wedges.

MARINATED COURGETTES AND MUSHROOMS

2 large courgettes, sliced
100 g (4 oz) mushrooms, chopped
5 ml (1 tsp) olive oil
10 ml (2 tsp) lime juice
5 ml (1 tsp) chopped fresh mint
freshly ground black pepper
lime wedges

Marinate the courgettes and mushrooms in the oil, lime juice, mint and black pepper for 30 minutes, or longer if possible. Serve on individual plates garnished with the lime wedges.

MEDITERRANEAN SALAD

1 beef tomato
75 g (3 oz) Feta cheese
fresh basil leaves
juice of ½ lemon
freshly ground black pepper

Slice the tomato and arrange on individual plates. Cut the Feta cheese into small cubes and place on top. Tear the basil leaves into pieces and scatter on top of the salad. Squeeze the lemon juice and grind some black pepper over the salad.

CARROT AND TUNA WITH ORANGES

100 g (4 oz) carrots, grated
1 tin tuna in brine, drained
1 large orange, peeled and segmented
juice of ½ orange
10 ml (2 tsp) white wine vinegar
3 ml (½ tsp) mustard
freshly ground black pepper

Flake the tuna and mix with the grated carrots. Arrange on individual plates and put the orange segments on top. Mix together the orange juice, white wine vinegar, mustard and black pepper and spoon over the salad.

CHICKEN WITH MANGO

2 chicken breast fillets, cooked
1 mango
watercress
10 ml (2 tsp) white wine vinegar
10 ml (2 tsp) lemon juice
3 ml (½ tsp) mustard
freshly ground black pepper

Cut the skin from the mango and cut the flesh into slices. Cut the chicken into pieces and mix with the mango. Arrange the watercress on individual plates with the chicken and mango on top. Mix the white wine vinegar with the lemon juice and mustard and spoon over the chicken and mango. Grind some black pepper over the salad.

CHICORY AND TUNA WITH KIWI FRUIT

1 large head chicory
1 small tin tuna in brine, drained
1 kiwi fruit, peeled and cut into pieces
*5 ml (1 tsp) chopped fresh chives or 3 ml (½ tsp) dried mixed
    herbs*

10 ml (2 tsp) reduced calorie mayonnaise
10 ml (2 tsp) low fat natural yogurt
freshly ground black pepper

Flake the tuna and mix with the herbs, mayonnaise, yogurt and black pepper. Cut the chicory leaves into rings and put on individual plates. Spoon the tuna on top of the chicory then arrange the pieces of kiwi fruit on the salad.

GARDEN SALAD

2 medium carrots, grated
1 stick celery, cut thinly
piece of cucumber, cut into wedges
2 medium tomatoes, cut into wedges
1 large pear, cut into small pieces
lemon juice
freshly ground black pepper

Put the grated carrot on individual plates. Arrange the celery, cucumber, tomato and pear on top of the carrot. Squeeze some lemon juice over the salad and add some freshly ground black pepper.

SPRING SALAD

crisp lettuce leaves
100 g (4 oz) sweetcorn
2 hard-boiled eggs, quartered
10 ml (2 tsp) pumpkin seeds
10 ml (2 tsp) reduced calorie mayonnaise
freshly ground black pepper

Shred the lettuce leaves and arrange on individual plates. Mix together the sweetcorn, pumpkin seeds and mayonnaise and put on top of the lettuce. Arrange the eggs on the salad and add some freshly ground black pepper.

MANGETOUT WITH RED PEPPER

100 g (4 oz) mangetout, lightly cooked
1 medium red pepper, cut into pieces
10 ml (2 tsp) chopped fresh mint
15 ml (1 tbsp) low fat natural yogurt
freshly ground black pepper

Arrange the mangetout and red pepper on individual plates. Mix together the yogurt and mint and spoon on to the salad. Add some freshly ground black pepper.

PASTA AND BEAN SALAD

100 g (4 oz) cooked pasta shapes
100 g (4 oz) broad beans, lightly cooked
2 medium tomatoes, cut into wedges
75 g (3 oz) seedless grapes
10 ml (2 tsp) reduced calorie mayonnaise
10 ml (2 tsp) low fat natural yogurt
cayenne pepper

Mix together the mayonnaise and yogurt and coat the pasta shapes, broad beans and grapes with the dressing. Arrange on individual plates. Garnish with the tomato wedges and dust the salad with cayenne pepper.

RED CABBAGE AND APPLE MAYONNAISE

wedge of red cabbage, finely shredded
2 apples, cored and cut into small pieces
10 ml (2 tsp) sesame seeds
10 ml (2 tsp) reduced calorie mayonnaise
10 ml (2 tsp) low fat natural yogurt
5 ml (1 tsp) chopped fresh mint
freshly ground black pepper

Mix together the red cabbage and apple and coat with the combined mayonnaise, yogurt and mint. Arrange on individual plates. Scatter the sesame seeds and grind some black pepper on to the salad.

WATERCRESS AND BEAN SALAD

watercress
220 g (8 oz) cooked red kidney beans
2 spring onions, cut into small pieces
5 ml (1 tsp) wine vinegar
15 ml (1 tbsp) freshly squeezed orange juice
freshly ground black pepper

Arrange the watercress on individual plates and add the beans and spring onions. Mix together the vinegar, orange juice and black pepper and spoon over the salad.

CAESAR SALAD

crispy lettuce leaves
2 slices wholemeal bread, crusts removed
4 anchovy fillets, soaked in milk to reduce saltiness
2 hard-boiled eggs, quartered
25 g (1 oz) freshly grated Parmesan cheese
juice of ½ lemon
freshly ground black pepper

Cut the bread into small squares. Bake for 15–20 minutes in a preheated oven, Gas Mark 6 (200C/400F). Arrange the lettuce leaves on individual plates. Add the hard-boiled egg quarters, anchovy fillets and croutons. Add the lemon juice, black pepper and Parmesan cheese.

SPINACH, MELON AND FETA CHEESE SALAD

young spinach leaves
½ Cantaloup melon
75 g (3 oz) Feta cheese
8 green olives

juice of ½ lemon
freshly ground black pepper

Put the spinach leaves on individual plates. Cut the melon and Feta cheese into cubes and arrange on the spinach. Add the lemon juice and black pepper and garnish with the olives.

CURRIED POTATOES AND PETITS POIS

300 g (10 oz) new potatoes, cooked and cut into small pieces
100 g (4 oz) petits pois, cooked
50 g (2 oz) sultanas
5 ml (1 tsp) garam masala or curry powder
few drops chilli sauce
125 g (5 oz) low fat natural yogurt
5 ml (1 tsp) chopped fresh chives
freshly ground black pepper

Mix together the garam masala, chilli sauce, yogurt and chives. Add the cooled potatoes and petits pois and the sultanas and coat them with the dressing. Arrange the potato salad on individual plates and add some freshly ground black pepper.

RUSSIAN SALAD

75 g (3 oz) cooked beetroot
75 g (3 oz) cooked potatoes
75 g (3 oz) cooked carrots
75 g (3 oz) cooked petits pois
10 ml (2 tsp) reduced calorie mayonnaise
5 ml (1 tsp) lemon juice
5 ml (1 tsp) horseradish sauce
freshly ground black pepper

Allow the vegetables to cool. Mix together the mayonnaise, lemon juice and horseradish sauce. Cut the potatoes and carrots into small pieces then add them with the petits pois to the dressing. Stir gently to coat the vegetables. Grate the

beetroot and arrange on serving dishes. Put the salad on top
of the beetroot and add some freshly ground black pepper.

ASPARAGUS ROLLS

12 cooked asparagus spears
6 slices Parma ham, or other dried ham
radicchio or other salad leaves
lemon juice
lemon wedges
freshly grated Parmesan cheese
freshly ground black pepper

Lay 2 asparagus spears on each slice of Parma ham and roll
into cigar shapes. Arrange the radicchio on serving dishes and
put the asparagus rolls on top. Squeeze some lemon juice
and grind some black pepper onto the asparagus rolls and
garnish with the lemon wedges. The Parmesan cheese may
be added at the table.

TUNA AND LEEK SALAD

1 tin tuna in brine, drained
2 medium leeks, cut into 4-inch sections and cleaned
10 ml (2 tsp) reduced calorie mayonnaise
10 ml (2 tsp) low fat natural yogurt
freshly ground black pepper
lemon wedges

Simmer the leeks in boiling water for about 8 minutes then
drain well and leave to cool. Flake the tuna and mix with the
mayonnaise and yogurt. Arrange the leeks on plates and pile
the tuna on top. Grind some black pepper onto the salad and
garnish with the lemon wedges.

MUSHROOMS A LA GRECQUE

220 g (8 oz) mushrooms
1 medium onion

1 clove garlic
2 medium tomatoes
1 red pepper
5 ml (1 tsp) chopped fresh parsley or 3 ml (½ tsp) dried mixed
    herbs
freshly ground black pepper and salt
black olives

Chop the mushrooms, onion, garlic, tomatoes and red pepper. Put the onion, garlic and tomatoes into a pan with a little water. Simmer over a medium heat for 10 minutes adding more water if necessary, then add all other ingredients except the olives and cook for a further 5 minutes. Garnish with the olives.

EGGS FLORENTINE

220 g (8 oz) fresh spinach
5 ml (1 tsp) Nam Pla fish sauce
chilli sauce – to taste
2 eggs
freshly ground black pepper

Clean the spinach then put it into a pan with a little water and cook for about 2 minutes. Drain the water from the spinach then add the fish sauce and the chilli sauce to the spinach and keep warm. Meanwhile, poach the eggs in some lightly salted boiling water. Arrange the spinach on individual plates with the poached egg on top of the spinach and grind some black pepper on to the egg. Serve with triangles of toast.

SMOKED FISH PATE

100 g (4 oz) smoked mackerel, smoked salmon or smoked trout
100 g (4 oz) low fat cottage cheese
10 ml (2 tsp) lemon juice
freshly ground black pepper

salad leaves
2 lemon wedges

Put the smoked fish, cottage cheese, lemon juice and black pepper into a food processor and whizz until smooth. Serve on individual plates garnished with salad leaves and lemon wedges. Serve with a wedge of wholemeal bread.

THAI PORK

150 g (6 oz) minced pork
1 small onion, finely chopped
50 g (2 oz) small mushrooms, finely sliced
2 medium tomatoes, skinned and chopped
125 ml (5 fl oz) water
5 ml (1 tsp) ground coriander
10 ml (2 tsp) Nam Pla fish sauce
5 ml (1 tsp) soy sauce
freshly ground black pepper
Iceberg lettuce leaves

Put the minced pork, onion, tomatoes, ground coriander and water into a saucepan and cook over a medium heat for about 20 minutes or until the meat is cooked, adding the mushrooms for the last 5 minutes. Reduce the liquid if necessary. Add the fish sauce, soy sauce and black pepper and mix thoroughly. Serve the meat and the lettuce leaves on separate dishes. Each person should put spoonfuls of meat into the lettuce leaves which should then be rolled up.

STUFFED TOMATOES

2 beef tomatoes
75 g (3 oz) lentils, soaked, cooked as directed and cooled
50 g (2 oz) sultanas
2 spring onions, chopped
5 ml (1 tsp) chopped fresh parsley
juice of ½ lemon
freshly ground black pepper

Slice the top off the tomato and scoop out the flesh. Mix all the other ingredients with the tomato flesh then pile into the tomatoes. Serve garnished with some salad leaves.

VEGETABLE KEBABS

1 large courgette
1 large onion
1 medium red pepper
8 small mushrooms
10 ml (2 tsp) lemon juice
5 ml (1 tsp) olive oil
5 ml (1 tsp) chopped fresh parsley or 3 ml (1/2 tsp) dried mixed
   herbs
freshly ground black pepper
2 lemon wedges

Soak four 6-inch kebab sticks in water for 30 minutes to prevent burning when cooking the kebabs. Cut the vegetables to make 4 kebabs. Mix the lemon juice, olive oil, herbs and black pepper to make a marinade and put the kebabs in the marinade for about 40 minutes. Grill the kebabs, turning frequently. Serve garnished with lemon wedges.

AUBERGINE WITH MOZZARELLA

1 medium aubergine
2 medium tomatoes
1/2 Mozzarella cheese
3 ml (1/2 tsp) dried mixed herbs
freshly ground black pepper

Roast the aubergine whole in a preheated oven, Gas Mark 6 (200C/400F) for about 30 minutes, turning occasionally. Cut the ends from the aubergine then slice in half lengthways. Slice the tomatoes and the mozzarella cheese and arrange on the aubergine halves. Add the herbs and black pepper and place under a hot grill for a few minutes until golden.

EGG MAYONNAISE WITH PRAWNS AND GRAPES

2 hard-boiled eggs
75 g (3 oz) cooked prawns
75 g (3 oz) seedless grapes
10 ml (2 tsp) reduced calorie mayonnaise
10 ml (2 tsp) low fat natural yogurt
cayenne pepper
2 lemon wedges

Cut the eggs in half and place, yolk down, on individual plates. Mix together the prawns, grapes, mayonnaise and yogurt, and arrange on top of the eggs. Add some cayenne pepper and serve garnished with lemon wedges.

MUSHROOM AND PEPPER OMELETTE

100 g (4 oz) mushrooms
1 small green pepper
1 small red pepper
5 ml (1 tsp) chopped fresh parsley or 3 ml (½ tsp) dried mixed
  herbs
3 large eggs
5 ml (1 tsp) olive or sunflower oil
freshly ground black pepper and salt

Cut the green and red peppers lengthways and remove the seeds. Slice the mushrooms. Grill the peppers and the mushrooms for 5–10 minutes, turning to cook evenly. Whisk the eggs with a little water and some black pepper and salt. Add the herbs. Heat the oil in a frying pan and add the eggs. Cook until the omelette is set. Arrange the grilled mushrooms and peppers on the omelette. Fold over and cut in half. Serve on individual plates garnished with a sprig of parsley.

MANGETOUT AND HAM OMELETTE

50 g (2 oz) mangetout, lightly cooked
50 g (2 oz) cooked ham, shredded

5 ml (1 tsp) chopped fresh dill or 3 ml (½ tsp) dried mixed herbs
3 large eggs
5 ml (1 tsp) olive or sunflower oil
freshly ground black pepper and salt

Whisk the eggs with a little water and some black pepper and salt. Add the herbs. Heat the oil in a frying pan and add the eggs. Cook until the omelette is set. Arrange the mangetout and ham on the omelette. Fold over and cut in half. Serve on individual plates garnished with a sprig of dill.

ROAST VEGETABLES

1 medium aubergine
1 red pepper
1 green pepper
1 medium onion
juice of ½ lemon
freshly ground black pepper

Roast the vegetables whole in a preheated oven, Gas Mark 6 (200C/400F), for about 40 minutes, turning 2 or 3 times. Put the red and green peppers into a food bag and leave for about 5 minutes, then peel the skins, remove the seeds and cut each pepper into half lengthways. Cut the ends from the aubergine then cut into half lengthways. Cut the skin from the onion and cut into quarters. Arrange the vegetables on individual plates and add the lemon juice and black pepper.

BAKED POTATO WITH PIQUANT MUSHROOMS

2 large baking potatoes
100 g (4 oz) mushrooms, chopped
2 medium tomatoes, skinned and chopped
1 clove garlic, finely chopped
2 spring onions, shredded
chilli sauce – to taste
freshly ground black pepper and salt

Bake the potatoes. Cook the mushrooms, tomatoes and garlic with a little water in a pan over a medium heat for 8 minutes. Reduce the liquid. Stir in the spring onions, chilli sauce and black pepper and salt. Cut the potatoes lengthways and pile the piquant mushrooms into the potatoes.

BAKED POTATOES WITH AUBERGINE PUREE

2 large baking potatoes
1 large aubergine
15 ml (1 tbsp) lemon juice
75 g (3 oz) low fat cottage cheese
cayenne pepper

Bake the potatoes. Roast the aubergine for about 40 minutes in a preheated oven, Gas Mark 6 (200C/400F). Cut the aubergine in half and scoop out the pulp. Purée it in a food processor or blender with the lemon juice and cottage cheese. Cut the potatoes lengthways and spoon the aubergine purée into the potatoes. Add a little cayenne pepper.

AVOCADO WITH ORANGE

1 small avocado
1 large orange
10 ml (2 tsp) toasted sesame seeds
juice of ½ lemon
salad leaves

Arrange the salad leaves on individual plates. Peel the orange and cut into segments, removing the pith. Cut the avocado into half, peel and cut the flesh into cubes. Arrange the avocado and orange on the salad leaves and spoon the lemon juice over the avocado to retain its colour. Garnish with the toasted sesame seeds.

BAKED TOMATOES

2 large tomatoes
1 clove garlic, finely chopped
25 g (1 oz) chopped almonds
10 ml (2 tsp) chopped fresh parsley
5 ml (1 tsp) olive or sunflower oil
freshly ground black pepper and salt

Cut the tomatoes in half and put them cut-side up in an ovenproof dish. Mix the rest of the ingredients together and put the mixture onto the tomato halves. Bake in a preheated oven, Gas Mark 6 (200C/400F), for about 20 minutes.

COURGETTES WITH SEAFOOD

2 large courgettes
1 small onion, finely chopped
50g (2 oz) mushrooms, finely chopped
100 g (4 oz) white fish fillet, skin removed
50 g (2 oz) cooked prawns
5 ml (1 tsp) chopped fresh dill or 3 ml ($\frac{1}{2}$ tsp) dried mixed herbs
5 ml (1 tsp) Nam Pla fish sauce
chilli sauce – to taste
125 ml (5 fl oz) water
freshly ground black pepper

Cut the ends from the courgettes and cut lengthways. Scoop out the seeds and pulp with a teaspoon, taking care not to break the courgettes, and reserve. Cook the courgettes in boiling, salted water for 8 minutes. Drain and keep warm. In another pan, cook the onion in the water over a medium heat for 5 minutes. Add the mushrooms, courgette seeds and pulp and white fish and cook for a further 8 minutes. Reduce the liquid to about 10 ml (2 tsp). Add the prawns, herbs, fish sauce, chilli sauce and black pepper and heat through. Put the courgettes on individual plates and spoon the seafood mixture onto the courgettes. Garnish with sprigs of dill.

BROCCOLI MORNAY

220 g (8 oz) broccoli, lightly cooked
2 hard-boiled eggs, sliced
125 g (5 fl oz) low fat natural yogurt
75 g (3 oz) low fat cheese, grated
freshly ground black pepper

Put the cooked broccoli and hard-boiled eggs in an ovenproof dish. Spoon over the yogurt and add the grated cheese and black pepper. Bake in a preheated oven, Gas Mark 6 (200C/400F), for about 15 minutes then put under a hot grill for a few moments.

TOMATO AND OLIVE CROSTINI

4 thin slices crusty bread
1 clove garlic, peeled and cut into half
4 medium tomatoes
fresh basil leaves, torn into pieces
8 black olives
freshly ground black pepper

Slice the tomatoes and put under a hot grill for a few minutes, turning once. Toast the bread, then rub with the cut clove of garlic. Arrange the tomatoes on the toasted bread then add the basil, olives and black pepper.

HAM AND CHEESE CROSTINI

4 thin slices crusty bread
4 slices Parma ham, or other dried ham
100 g (4 oz) low fat cheese, grated
10 ml (2 tsp) chopped fresh parsley
freshly ground black pepper

Toast the bread. Arrange the ham on the toasted bread and then add the cheese. Put under a hot grill for a few moments until golden. Add the parsley and black pepper.

Pasta and Rice

PASTA SICILIANA

150 g (6 oz) pasta shapes
1 medium onion, chopped
1 clove garlic, chopped
100 g (4 oz) mushrooms, cut into small pieces
1 medium aubergine, cut into pieces
1 small red pepper, cut into small pieces
220 g (8 oz) tomatoes, skinned and chopped
5 ml (1 tsp) tomato purée
125 ml (5 fl oz) water
5 ml (1 tsp) chopped fresh basil or 3 ml (½ tsp) dried mixed herbs
freshly ground black pepper
½ Mozzarella cheese, cut into pieces or 75 g (3 oz) low fat cheese,
    grated

Cook the pasta as directed. Put the tomatoes, tomato purée and water into a large saucepan and cook the onion, garlic and aubergine over a medium heat for 10 minutes. Add the mushrooms, red pepper and herbs and cook for a further 5 minutes adding more water if necessary. Mix the cooked pasta into the sauce then add the cheese and black pepper and stir well.

PASTA AMATRICIANA

150 g (6 oz) pasta
1 medium onion, chopped
1 clove garlic, chopped
100 g (4 oz) mushrooms, cut into small pieces
1 small red pepper, cut into small pieces
100 g (4 oz) bacon, cut into small pieces
100 g (4 oz) tomatoes, skinned and chopped
5 ml (1 tsp) tomato purée
125 ml (5 fl oz) water

few drops of chilli sauce – to taste
5 ml (1 tsp) chopped fresh parsley or 3 ml (½ tsp) dried mixed
*   herbs*
freshly ground black pepper

Cook the pasta as directed. Put the tomatoes, tomato purée and water into a large saucepan and add the onion, garlic and bacon. Cook over a medium heat for 10 minutes. Add the mushrooms, green pepper, chilli sauce, herbs and black pepper and cook for a further 5 minutes adding more water if necessary. Put the cooked pasta onto individual plates and spoon over the sauce.

PASTA WITH SMOKED SALMON

150 g (6 oz) pasta
100 g (4 oz) smoked salmon – end cuts are suitable
1 small onion, finely chopped
100 g (4 oz) mushrooms, sliced
10 ml (2 tsp) Nam Pla fish sauce
5 ml (1 tsp) chopped fresh dill or 3 ml (½ tsp) dried mixed herbs
125 ml (5 fl oz) low fat single cream
freshly ground black pepper

Cook the pasta as directed. Cook the onion and mushrooms in a little water for 8 minutes. Reduce the liquid if necessary. Stir in the fish sauce, herbs and black pepper. Cut the smoked salmon into small pieces. Add the cream and smoked salmon and heat through. Put the pasta onto individual dishes and spoon over the sauce. Add some freshly ground black pepper.

PASTA WITH TUNA AND WALNUTS

150 g (6 oz) pasta
1 tin tuna in brine, drained and flaked
50 g (2 oz) shelled walnuts
1 medium onion, chopped
fresh basil leaves, torn into pieces
5 ml (1 tsp) Nam Pla fish sauce

125 ml (5 fl oz) low fat single cream
cayenne pepper

Cook the pasta as directed. Cook the onion in a little water for 8 minutes. Reduce the liquid if necessary. Add the tuna, basil, fish sauce and cream and heat through. Reserve 2 walnut halves for a garnish and chop the remaining walnuts. Stir into the sauce. Put the pasta on to individual dishes and spoon over the sauce. Add some cayenne pepper and garnish with the walnut halves.

PASTA WITH PRAWNS AND PEPPERS

150 g (6 oz) pasta shapes
100 g (4 oz) cooked prawns
1 tin chopped tomatoes
1 medium onion, finely chopped
1 small red pepper, chopped
1 small green pepper, chopped
fresh basil leaves, torn into pieces
chilli sauce – to taste
freshly ground black pepper and salt

Cook the pasta as directed. Put the chopped tomatoes and onion into a large pan and cook over a medium heat for 8 minutes. Add the red and green peppers, chilli sauce and black pepper and salt and cook for a further 5 minutes. Stir the cooked pasta, prawns and basil into the sauce, reserving a few basil leaves for a garnish. Serve on individual plates garnished with the basil leaves.

PASTA WITH HAM AND PETITS POIS

150 g (6 oz) pasta
100 g (4 oz) cooked ham, shredded
100 g (4 oz) mushrooms, chopped
1 medium onion, finely chopped
100 g (4 oz) petits pois

5 ml (1 tsp) chopped fresh thyme or 3 ml (½ tsp) dried mixed
  herbs
10 ml (2 tsp) Nam Pla fish sauce
3 ml (½ tsp) mustard
75 ml (3 fl oz) low fat single cream
freshly ground black pepper

Cook the pasta as directed. Cook the onion and petits pois in some water for 8 minutes. Add the mushrooms and herbs and cook for a further 5 minutes. Reduce the liquid if necessary. Add the fish sauce, mustard, cream and ham and heat through. Put the pasta on individual plates and spoon over the sauce. Add some freshly ground black pepper.

PASTA WITH PASTRAMI

150 g (6 oz) pasta
75 g (3 oz) pastrami, cut into strips
1 small red pepper, chopped
1 small green pepper, chopped
1 medium onion, chopped
2 medium tomatoes, skinned and chopped
chilli sauce – to taste
125 ml (5 fl oz) water
fresh basil leaves, torn into pieces or 5 ml (1 tsp) dried mixed herbs
freshly ground black pepper

Cook the pasta as directed. Put the onion, tomatoes and water into a pan and cook over a medium heat for 10 minutes. Add the red and green peppers and cook for a further 5 minutes. Reduce the liquid if necessary. Add the pastrami, chilli sauce, herbs and black pepper and heat through, stirring occasionally. Put the pasta on individual plates and spoon over the sauce.

PASTA WITH MUSHROOMS

150 g (6 oz) pasta
220 g (8 oz) mushrooms, chopped (try to use 2 or 3 different
  varieties)

1 *medium onion, chopped*
1 *clove garlic, finely chopped*
5 *ml (1 tsp) chopped fresh parsley or 3 ml (½ tsp) dried mixed*
  herbs
10 *ml (2 tsp) Nam Pla fish sauce*
125 *ml (5 fl oz) water*
75 *ml (3 fl oz) low fat single cream*
freshly ground black pepper

Cook the pasta as directed. Put the onion, garlic and water into a pan and cook over a medium heat for 5 minutes. Add the mushrooms and herbs and cook for a further 5 minutes. Reduce the liquid if necessary. Add the fish sauce, cream and black pepper and heat through. Put the pasta on individual plates and spoon over the sauce.

VEGETABLE PILAU

220 *g (8 oz) mushrooms, sliced*
2 *medium courgettes, sliced*
1 *medium red pepper, chopped*
100 *g (4 oz) petits pois*
1 *medium onion, chopped*
1 *clove garlic, chopped*
1 *tin chopped tomatoes*
25 *g (1 oz) sultanas*
10 *ml (2 tsp) ground coriander*
5 *ml (1 tsp) ground cumin*
chilli sauce – to taste
15 *ml (1 tbsp) lemon juice*
freshly ground black pepper and salt
150 *g (6 oz) basmati rice*
lemon wedges – to garnish

Cook the rice as indicated. Put the onion, garlic and tomatoes into a large saucepan and cook over a medium heat for 10 minutes. Add all other ingredients except the rice and cook for a further 10 minutes, stirring well. Reduce the liquid to a sauce just coating the vegetables. Stir in the cooked rice and serve garnished with lemon wedges.

PRAWNS WITH RICE

220 g (8 oz) prawns
1 medium onion, chopped
1 clove garlic, chopped
220 g (8 oz) tomatoes, skinned and chopped
125 ml (5 fl oz) water
chilli sauce – to taste
1 bouquet garni or 3 ml (½ tsp) dried mixed herbs
150 g (6 oz) long-grain rice
freshly ground black pepper and salt

Cook the rice as directed. Cook the onion, garlic and tomatoes with the water and herbs in a medium saucepan for 10 minutes. Add the chilli sauce and black pepper and salt. Reduce the liquid if necessary. Add the prawns and heat through gently. Stir in the cooked rice.

PAELLA

100 g (4 oz) cooked prawns
100 g (4 oz) cooked mussels, out of the shell
4 squid, prepared and cut into rings
1 medium onion, chopped
1 clove garlic, finely chopped
100 g (4 oz) petits pois
1 medium red pepper, chopped
100 g (4 oz) mushrooms, chopped
*10 ml (2 tsp) chopped fresh parsley or 5 ml (1 tsp) dried mixed
    herbs*
10 ml (2 tsp) Nam Pla fish sauce
few strands saffron or 3 ml (½ tsp) turmeric powder
150 g (6 oz) long-grain rice
freshly ground black pepper
large prawns and mussels in their shells for garnish – optional
lemon wedges

Cook the rice as directed in a medium pan with the saffron or turmeric. Put the onion, garlic and petits pois into a large frying pan with some water and cook over a medium heat for 10 minutes, stirring occasionally. Add the squid, red pepper, mushrooms, herbs and black pepper and cook for a further 5 minutes. Reduce the liquid if necessary. Stir in the cooked rice and fish sauce and then the cooked prawns and mussels. Garnish with the large prawns and mussels and lemon wedges.

JAMBALAYA

2 chicken breast fillets, skin removed, cut into small pieces
1 tin chopped tomatoes
1 medium onion, chopped
100 g (4 oz) mushrooms, chopped
1 medium red pepper, chopped
100 g (4 oz) cooked red kidney beans
100 g (4 oz) sweetcorn
10 ml (2 tsp) chopped fresh parsley or 5 ml (1 tsp) dried mixed herbs
chilli sauce – to taste
150 g (6 oz) brown rice
freshly ground black pepper and salt
lime wedges

Cook the rice as directed. Put the chicken, chopped tomatoes and onion into a large pan and cook over a medium heat for about 15 minutes, stirring occasionally. Add the mushrooms and red pepper and cook for a further 5 minutes. Stir in the cooked rice, red kidney beans, sweetcorn, herbs, chilli sauce and black pepper and salt. Garnish wth lime wedges.

Vegetarian

SWEET AND SOUR COURGETTES AND PEPPERS

2 large courgettes, sliced
1 medium red pepper, chopped

1 *medium green pepper, chopped*
1 *medium onion, finely chopped*
15 *ml (1 tbsp) olive oil*
10 *ml (2 tsp) wine vinegar*
10 *ml (2 tsp) soy sauce*
10 *ml (2 tsp) clear honey*
juice of 1 large orange
25 *g (1 oz) pine kernels*
25 *g (1 oz) sultanas*
freshly ground black pepper

Heat the olive oil in a large saucepan and cook the onion over a medium heat for 5 minutes. Add the courgettes and red and green peppers then add the wine vinegar, soy sauce, honey, freshly squeezed orange juice and black pepper and cook for a further 5 minutes mixing well. Serve with the pine kernels and sultanas scattered over the vegetables.

SPICY VEGETABLES

1 *large aubergine*
2 *medium courgettes*
1 *medium onion*
100 *g (4 oz) mushrooms*
15 *ml (1 tbsp) olive oil*
30 *ml (2 tbsp) lime juice*
5 *ml (1 tsp) paprika*
5 *ml (1 tsp) ground cumin*
10 *ml (2 tsp) ground coriander*
chilli sauce – to taste
freshly ground black pepper and salt

Cut the aubergine and courgettes into small pieces and chop the onion and mushrooms. Put the olive oil in a large pan and heat. Add the onion and cook gently for 5 minutes then add the ground spices and stir. Pour 220 ml (8 fl oz) water into the pan and add the aubergine and courgettes. Stir then cover the pan and simmer for about 10 minutes. Add the mushrooms and cook for a further 5 minutes then reduce the liquid to a sauce just coating the vegetables. Add the lime juice, chilli sauce and pepper and salt.

BEAN RAGOUT

125 g (5 oz) cooked red kidney beans
125 g (5 oz) cooked white haricot beans
125 g (5 oz) cooked green Lima or broad beans
1 large onion, chopped
1 clove garlic, chopped
100 g (4 oz) mushrooms, chopped
1 red pepper, chopped
1 tin chopped tomatoes
5 ml (1 tsp) soy sauce
10 ml (2 tsp) chopped fresh mint or 5 ml (1 tsp) dried mixed herbs
freshly ground black pepper

Cook the onion and garlic with the tomatoes, soy sauce, herbs and black pepper in a large saucepan for 5 minutes then add the mushrooms and red pepper and cook for a further 5 minutes. Add the beans and heat through thoroughly, reducing the liquid if necessary.

RATATOUILLE

1 medium onion
1 clove garlic
1 large aubergine
2 medium courgettes
1 large red pepper
100 g (4 oz) mushrooms
1 tin chopped tomatoes
chilli sauce – to taste
5 ml (1 tsp) chopped fresh thyme or 3 ml (½ tsp) dried mixed herbs
1 bay leaf
freshly ground black pepper and salt

Clean and chop all the vegetables. Put the onion, garlic and aubergine into a saucepan with the chopped tomatoes, chilli sauce and herbs. Cook over a medium heat for about 10 minutes. Add the courgettes, red pepper, mushrooms and black pepper and salt and cook for a further 5 minutes.

DAUBE D'AUBERGINES

1 large aubergine, cut into small pieces
1 medium onion, chopped
100 g (4 oz) mushrooms, chopped
1 large tin chopped tomatoes
125 ml (5 fl oz) water
5 ml (1 tsp) lemon juice
5 ml (1 tsp) chopped fresh parsley or 3 ml (½ tsp) dried mixed
    herbs
2 cloves garlic, finely chopped
freshly ground black pepper and salt
black olives to garnish

In a large saucepan, cook the aubergines and onion in the chopped tomatoes and water for 10 minutes. Add the mushrooms, lemon juice, herbs, garlic and salt and pepper and cook for a further 5 minutes. Garnish with black olives.

VEGETABLE GOULASH

1 large onion
1 large potato
1 large carrot
1 medium turnip
1 large parsnip
150 g (6 oz) petits pois
150 g (6 oz) sweetcorn
1 bouquet garni or 5 ml (1 tsp) dried mixed herbs
15 ml (1 tbsp) tomato purée
300 ml (10 fl oz) water
15 ml (1 tbsp) paprika
freshly ground black pepper and salt

Prepare all vegetables by peeling or cleaning as appropriate then cut into pieces. Put in a large saucepan, leaving the petits pois and sweetcorn to be added later. Mix together the tomato purée, water, paprika, black pepper and salt and pour over the vegetables, adding the herbs. Bring to the boil and simmer over a medium heat for 20–30 minutes or until the vegetables are cooked, reducing the liquid if necessary. Add the petits pois and sweetcorn for the last 5 minutes.

BAKED FENNEL

2 medium fennel bulbs
1 medium onion, chopped
1 clove garlic, finely chopped
2 medium tomatoes, skinned and chopped
*5 ml (1 tsp) chopped fresh parsley or 3 ml (¹/₂ tsp) dried mixed
    herbs*
10 ml (2 tsp) olive or sunflower oil
125 ml (5 fl oz) water or wine and water, mixed
freshly ground black pepper and salt

Trim and cut the fennel in half lengthways. Heat the oil in a medium pan and cook the onion and garlic over a medium heat for 5 minutes. Add the fennel and cook for a further 5 minutes. Add the tomatoes, herbs, wine and water and black pepper and salt. Cover the pan and simmer, stirring occasionally for about 20 minutes.

VEGETABLES GITANA

150 g (6 oz) cooked chick peas
150 g (6 oz) cooked green Lima or broad beans
1 medium onion, chopped
1 clove garlic, finely chopped
2 medium tomatoes, skinned and chopped
2 small pears, cored and chopped
15 ml (1 tbsp) wine vinegar
5 ml (1 tsp) paprika
3 ml (¹/₂ tsp) turmeric

10 ml (2 tsp) ground almonds
125 ml (5 fl oz) water
freshly ground black pepper and salt

Put the onion, garlic, tomatoes, pears and water into a large pan and cook over a medium heat for 10 minutes, stirring occasionally. Add the wine vinegar, paprika, turmeric, ground almonds and pepper and salt and mix thoroughly. Add the chick peas and beans and simmer for about 5 minutes.

Fish

WHITE FISH WITH LEEKS

220 g (8 oz) skinless fillets of white fish
220 g (8 oz) leeks, cleaned and finely chopped
5 ml (1 tsp) chopped fresh dill or 3 ml (½ tsp) dried mixed herbs
10 ml (2 tsp) Nam Pla fish sauce
125 ml (5 fl oz) low fat single cream
freshly ground black pepper
300 ml (10 fl oz) water

Poach the leeks in the water in a large pan for 8 minutes. Cut the fish into small pieces. Add them to the leeks and cook for a further 8 minutes. Reduce the liquid if necessary. Add the herbs, fish sauce and black pepper. Gently stir the cream in until warm.

BAKED FISH WITH TOASTED ALMONDS

2 125 g (5 oz) fish steaks, such as swordfish, tuna or cod
1 medium onion, chopped
1 medium red pepper, finely chopped
10 ml (2 tsp) Nam Pla fish sauce
10 ml (2 tsp) lemon juice
5 ml (1 tsp) chopped fresh parsley or 3 ml (½ tsp) dried mixed herbs
5 ml (1 tsp) ground coriander

5 ml (1 tsp) olive or sunflower oil
75 ml (3 fl oz) water
freshly ground black pepper
50 g (2 oz) split almonds

Put the fish, onion and red pepper into an ovenproof dish.
Combine all other ingredients except the almonds, pour over
the fish, cover and bake in a preheated oven, Gas Mark 6
(200C/400F) for 20 minutes. Remove the lid and bake for a
further 5 minutes. Toast the split almonds until golden brown
and arrange on top of the fish.

WHITE FISH WITH TOMATOES AND PEAS

220 g (8 oz) skinless fillets of white fish
1 large tin chopped tomatoes
1 medium onion, chopped
100 g (4 oz) mushrooms, chopped
100 g (4 oz) fresh garden peas or frozen petits pois
100 g (4 oz) mangetout
10 ml (2 tsp) chopped fresh basil or 5 ml (1 tsp) dried mixed herbs
10 ml (2 tsp) Nam Pla fish sauce
freshly ground black pepper

Put the tomatoes and onion in a large pan and simmer over
a medium heat for 10 minutes. Cut the fish into small pieces.
Add the fish and all the other ingredients and cook for a
further 10 minutes stirring occasionally.

FISH PILAKI

220 g (8 oz) skinless fillets of white fish
2 sticks of celery, with leaves, chopped
1 medium onion, chopped
220 g (8 oz) tomatoes, skinned and chopped
10 ml (2 tsp) chopped fresh parsley or 5 ml (1 tsp) dried mixed
    herbs
10 ml (2 tsp) Nam Pla fish sauce
15 ml (1 tbsp) lemon juice

125 ml (5 fl oz) water
freshly ground black pepper
black olives for garnish

Put the onion, tomatoes and water into a saucepan and cook
over a medium heat for 5 minutes. Add the fish and celery,
simmer for about 10 minutes then break the fish into bite-
size pieces. Reduce the liquid if necessary. Stir in all the other
ingredients and heat through. Serve garnished with the olives.

FISH WITH PINE NUTS AND SULTANAS

300 g (10 oz) skinless fillets of white fish
1 medium onion, chopped
1 tin chopped tomatoes
10 ml (2 tsp) Nam Pla fish sauce
10 ml (2 tsp) chopped fresh parsley or 5 ml (1 tsp) dried mixed
    herbs
50 g (2 oz) pine nuts
50 g (2 oz) sultanas
freshly ground black pepper

Put the onion and the chopped tomatoes into a medium pan
and cook for 10 minutes. Add the fish, fish sauce, herbs and
black pepper and simmer for about 8 minutes adding the pine
nuts and sultanas for the last 2 or 3 minutes.

PRAWN KORMA

220 g (8 oz) cooked prawns
1 medium onion, chopped
100 g (4 oz) mushrooms, chopped
10 ml (2 tsp) vegetable oil
10 ml (2 tsp) ground coriander
5 ml (1 tsp) ground cumin
5 ml (1 tsp) ground turmeric
125 ml (5 fl oz) low fat natural yogurt
freshly ground black pepper and salt

Heat the oil in a pan then add the onion, coriander, cumin, turmeric and black pepper and salt. Cook over a medium heat for 10 minutes, stirring at first to amalgamate the spices. Add the mushrooms and cook for a further 5 minutes. Finally stir in the prawns and yogurt and heat through. Serve with rice.

PRAWNS WITH CASHEW NUTS

150 g (6 oz) cooked prawns
1 small red pepper, sliced
100 g (4 oz) mushrooms, sliced
2 spring onions, shredded
5 ml (1 tsp) wine vinegar
5 ml (1 tsp) soy sauce
5 ml (1 tsp) clear honey
juice of ½ orange
50 g (2 oz) cashew nuts
125 ml (5 fl oz) water
freshly ground black pepper and salt

Put the red pepper, mushrooms and water in a pan and cook over a medium heat for 8 minutes, reducing the liquid to 10 ml (2 tsp). Add the wine vinegar, soy sauce, honey, orange juice and black pepper and salt and mix thoroughly. Stir in the prawns, spring onions and cashew nuts and heat through.

SCAMPI PROVENCAL

300 g (10 oz) raw scampi
1 medium onion, chopped
1 clove garlic, chopped
100 g (4 oz) petits pois
100 g (4 oz) mushrooms, chopped
1 medium red pepper, chopped
1 tin chopped tomatoes
10 ml (2 tsp) chopped fresh parsley or 5 ml (1 tsp) dried mixed
    herbs
chilli sauce – to taste
freshly ground black pepper and salt

Put the onion, garlic, petits pois and chopped tomatoes into a large pan and simmer over a medium heat for about 10 minutes. Add all the other ingredients and cook for a further 5 minutes. Serve with rice.

SALMON PARCELS

2 125 g (5 oz) skinless fillets of salmon
10/12 large spinach leaves
100 g (4 oz) mushrooms, chopped
5 ml (1 tsp) chopped fresh dill or 3 ml (½ tsp) dried mixed herbs
10 ml (2 tsp) Nam Pla fish sauce
75 ml (3 fl oz) low fat single cream
freshly ground black pepper

Blanch the spinach leaves in boiling water for about 30 seconds, then dry with a paper towel. Wrap 5/6 leaves around each salmon fillet. Steam in a vegetable steamer over boiling water for 5 minutes. Meanwhile, put the mushrooms, herbs and a little water into a small pan and cook over a medium heat for 5 minutes. Reduce the liquid to about 15 ml (1 tbsp). Add the fish sauce, cream and black pepper and heat through. Place the salmon on individual plates and spoon the mushroom sauce around the fish.

TUNA KEBABS

300 g (10 oz) fresh tuna
1 small red pepper
1 small green pepper
olive oil
freshly ground black pepper
lime wedges

Soak 4 6-inch kebab sticks in water for 30 minutes to prevent burning when cooking the kebabs. Cut the tuna and the red and green peppers into cubes. Thread onto the kebab sticks. Brush with olive oil and grind some black pepper onto the kebabs. Grill for about 6–8 minutes, turning to cook evenly. Serve garnished with lime wedges.

Meat and Poultry

CHICKEN PROVENCAL

2 chicken breast fillets, skin removed
1 tin chopped tomatoes
1 medium onion
1 medium aubergine
100 g (4 oz) courgettes
50 g (2 oz) mushrooms
1 red pepper
50 g (2 oz) black olives
1 clove garlic
1 bouquet garni or 3 ml (½ tsp) dried mixed herbs
freshly ground black pepper and salt

Chop the onion, aubergine, courgettes, mushrooms and red pepper. Cut the chicken into small pieces. Put the onion, aubergine and courgettes into a large pan with the chicken, tomatoes, garlic and herbs. Cook for 20 minutes, stirring occasionally. Add other vegetables and black pepper and salt and cook for a further 10 minutes.

NORMANDY CHICKEN

2 chicken breast fillets, skin removed
100 g (4 oz) mushrooms, chopped
1 medium onion, chopped
300 ml (10 fl oz) cider
75 ml (3 fl oz) low fat single cream
5 ml (1 tsp) Nam Pla fish sauce
5 ml (1 tsp) chopped fresh tarragon or 3 ml (½ tsp) dried mixed
    herbs
freshly ground black pepper and salt

Put the chicken, onion and cider into a pan and poach for about 20 minutes. Add the mushrooms and herbs and cook for a further 5 minutes. Reduce the liquid to about 30 ml (2 tbsp) then add the pepper and salt, fish sauce and cream and heat through.

CHICKEN VILAO

2 chicken breast fillets, skin removed
1 medium red onion, chopped
2 medium potatoes
150 g (6 oz) broccoli
1 hard-boiled egg, quartered
5 ml (1 tsp) chopped fresh parsley or 3 ml (½ tsp) dried mixed
     herbs
10 ml (2 tsp) wine vinegar
10 ml (2 tsp) olive oil
freshly ground black pepper and salt

Boil the potatoes in their skins and cut into 1/2-inch rounds, and lightly cook the broccoli. Heat the olive oil in a medium pan and gently cook the chicken with the onion for about 20 minutes. Arrange the potatoes, broccoli and hard-boiled egg on individual plates and keep warm. Add the wine vinegar, herbs and freshly ground black pepper and salt to the chicken for a few moments then put the chicken on to the vegetables and spoon over the sauce.

CHICKEN VAL BON

2 chicken breast fillets, skin removed
1 medium onion, chopped
1 medium red pepper, chopped
150 g (6 oz) tomatoes, chopped
10 ml (2 tsp) tomato purée
50 g (2 oz) chorizo sausage, skinned and cut into small pieces
300 ml (10 fl oz) wine and water, mixed
juice of 1 large orange

5 ml (1 tsp) chopped fresh parsley or 3 ml (½ tsp) dried mixed
    herbs
3 ml (½ tsp) paprika
freshly ground black pepper and salt
black olives for garnish

Put the chicken, onion, garlic, chorizo sausage, tomatoes and
tomato purée into a large saucepan with the wine and water
and simmer over a medium heat for about 20 minutes. Add
the red pepper, herbs, paprika and black pepper and salt and
cook for a further 5 minutes, reducing the liquid if necessary.
Pour the freshly squeezed orange juice over the chicken and
serve garnished with the olives.

MOROCCAN CHICKEN

2 chicken breast fillets, skin removed
1 medium onion, chopped
220 g (8 oz) cooked chick peas
15 ml (1 tbsp) chopped fresh parsley
5 ml (1 tsp) ground cinnamon
3 ml (½ tsp) ground turmeric
3 ml (½ tsp) paprika
juice of 1 lemon
15 ml (1 tbsp) olive oil
125 ml (5 fl oz) water
50 g (2 oz) flaked almonds
freshly ground black pepper and salt

Put the chicken into a saucepan with all other ingredients
except the chick peas and the almonds. Cover, bring to the
boil and simmer for about 25 minutes or until the chicken is
tender, stirring occasionally and adding more water if necessary. Add the chick peas for the last 5 minutes. Garnish with
the flaked almonds and serve with rice or couscous.

CANTONESE CHICKEN

2 chicken breast fillets, skin removed, cut into small pieces
6 spring onions, chopped
1 red pepper, chopped
100 g (4 oz) mushrooms, chopped
100 g (4 oz) petits pois
10 ml (2 tsp) Nam Pla fish sauce
10 ml (2 tsp) soy sauce
10 ml (2 tsp) vegetable oil
125 ml (5 fl oz) water
freshly ground black pepper

Heat the vegetable oil in a large pan and cook the chicken for about 10 minutes, stirring to prevent sticking. Pour the water into the pan and add the red pepper, mushrooms and petits pois. Cook for a further 5 minutes then reduce the liquid. Add the fish sauce, soy sauce and black pepper and mix thoroughly. At the last moment stir in the chopped spring onions.

CHICKEN TIKKA

2 chicken breast fillets, skin removed
125 g (5 oz) low fat natural yogurt
1 medium onion, chopped
1 clove garlic, finely chopped
5 ml (1 tsp) ground coriander
3 ml (½ tsp) ground cumin
3 ml (½ tsp) ground turmeric
few drops of chilli sauce
15 ml (1 tbsp) lemon juice
lemon wedges

Cut the chicken into small pieces. Mix together all the other ingredients and put the chicken pieces into this marinade for at least 30 minutes or up to 4 hours if possible. Leave in the refrigerator until ready to cook. Take the chicken pieces out of the marinade and put on a wire rack over a baking tray.

Bake in a preheated oven, Gas Mark 8 (230C/450F), for about 30 minutes. Serve garnished with lemon wedges.

TROPICAL CHICKEN

2 chicken breast fillets, skin removed, cut into small pieces
1 medium red onion, chopped
1 medium red pepper, finely chopped
2 medium courgettes, grated
¼ fresh pineapple
25 g (1 oz) shredded coconut
25 g (1 oz) flaked almonds
chilli sauce – to taste
125 ml (5 fl oz) water
2 bay leaves
freshly ground black pepper and salt

Put the chicken, onion, bay leaves and water into a large pan and cook over a medium heat for 15 minutes. Add the red pepper and courgettes and cook for a further 5 minutes. Reduce the liquid if necessary. Add the pineapple, chilli sauce and black pepper and salt. Serve on individual plates and garnish with the coconut and almonds.

TURKEY KOFTAS

220 g (8 oz) minced turkey
1 small onion, grated
5 ml (1 tsp) garam masala or curry powder
5 ml (1 tsp) lemon juice
freshly ground black pepper and salt
cornflour

Soak 4 6-inch kebab sticks in water for 30 minutes to prevent burning when cooking. Mix all the ingredients except the cornflour together and separate into 8 balls. Flatten into a sausage shape, coat with cornflour then put 2 pieces of meat on to each kebab. Grill under a medium heat for about 10 minutes or until cooked, turning several times. Serve on shredded lettuce, garnished with lemon wedges.

MEXICAN TURKEY

300 g (10 oz) minced turkey
1 medium onion, chopped
1 tin chopped tomatoes
1 medium red pepper, chopped
100 g (4 oz) mushrooms, chopped
220 g (8 oz) cooked red kidney beans
100 g (4 oz) sweetcorn
chilli sauce – to taste
freshly ground black pepper and salt

Put the turkey, onion and tomatoes into a large pan and cook over a medium heat for about 20 minutes, stirring occasionally. Add all the other ingredients and cook for a further 5 minutes.

TURKEY WITH PEPPER SAUCE

300 g (10 oz) turkey breast fillets
1 medium onion, finely chopped
2 medium tomatoes, skinned and chopped
1 large red pepper, chopped
10 ml (2 tsp) tomato purée
50 g (2 oz) raisins
10 ml (2 tsp) chopped fresh tarragon or 5 ml (1 tsp) dried mixed
    herbs
125 ml (5 fl oz) water
freshly ground black pepper and salt

Grill the turkey breast fillets under a medium heat for about 20 minutes or until golden, turning occasionally. Meanwhile, put the onion, tomatoes and water into a pan and cook over a medium heat for 10 minutes. Add the red pepper, tomato purée, raisins, herbs and black pepper and salt and cook for a further 10 minutes, stirring to prevent sticking and adding more water if necessary. Put the turkey onto individual plates and spoon over the pepper sauce. Garnish with a sprig of tarragon.

TURKEY FLORENTINE

300 g (10 oz) turkey breast fillets
220 g (8 oz) fresh spinach
5 ml (1 tsp) Nam Pla fish sauce
olive oil
50 g (2 oz) low fat cheese, grated
freshly ground black pepper

Brush the turkey breast fillets with olive oil and grill for about 20 minutes, turning occasionally to cook evenly. Clean the spinach then put it into a pan with a little water and cook for about 2 minutes. Drain the water from the spinach then add the fish sauce. Put the spinach onto a heatproof plate and the turkey on top of the spinach. Add the black pepper and the cheese and put under a hot grill for a few moments until golden.

PORK IN RED WINE

220 g (8 oz) pork fillet, cut into bite-sized pieces
1 fennel bulb, trimmed, cored and cut into quarters
1 medium onion, chopped
1 clove garlic, chopped
100 g (4 oz) mushrooms, chopped
125 ml (5 fl oz) red wine
125 ml (5 fl oz) water
5 ml (1 tsp) chopped fresh parsley or 3 ml (½ tsp) dried mixed
   herbs
chilli sauce – to taste
freshly ground black pepper

Put the pork fillet, fennel, onion and garlic into a large saucepan and add the red wine, water, herbs, chilli sauce and black pepper. Cover the saucepan, bring to the boil then simmer over a medium heat for about 30 minutes or until the meat is tender, adding more wine or water if necessary. Add the mushrooms for the last 5 minutes.

PORK WITH MUSHROOM SAUCE

300g (10 oz) pork fillet, in one piece
300 ml (10 fl oz) water or white wine and water, mixed
100 g (4 oz) mushrooms, finely chopped
5 ml (1 tsp) chopped fresh chives or 3 ml (½ tsp) dried mixed herbs
3 ml (½ tsp) mustard
75 ml (3 fl oz) low fat single cream
freshly ground black pepper

Put the pork fillet in one piece in an ovenproof dish with the white wine and water. Cover and bake for 30 minutes in a preheated oven, Gas Mark 6 (200C/400F). Put the pork fillet onto a plate and keep warm. Pour the juices into a pan and add the mushrooms. Cook over a medium heat for 5 minutes. Reduce the liquid to about 30 ml (2 tbsp). Stir in the herbs, mustard, cream and black pepper. Cut the pork fillet into ¾ inch round slices. Arrange on individual plates and spoon over the mushroom sauce.

TURKISH LAMB

2 125 g (5 oz) lean lamb steaks
1 medium onion, chopped
1 small bunch spring onions, chopped
10 ml (2 tsp) chopped fresh dill or 5 ml (1 tsp) dried mixed herbs
15 ml (1 tbsp) olive oil
125 ml (5 fl oz) water
juice of 1 lemon
freshly ground black pepper and salt

Cut any excess fat from the lamb steaks. Put in a saucepan with all other ingredients. Cover, bring to the boil and simmer for about 25 minutes or until the lamb is tender, stirring occasionally and adding more water if necessary.

LAMB WITH COURGETTES

300 g (10 oz) minced lamb
2 large courgettes, sliced
1 medium onion, chopped
1 clove garlic, chopped
1 tin chopped tomatoes
5 ml (1 tsp) tomato purée
10 ml (2 tsp) ground coriander
10 ml (2 tsp) chopped fresh mint or 5 ml (1 tsp) mint sauce
freshly ground black pepper and salt

Put the lamb, onion, garlic and chopped tomatoes into a pan and cook over a medium heat for 20 minutes. Add the courgettes, tomato purée, coriander, mint and pepper and salt and cook for a further 10 minutes. Serve with rice or couscous.

BEEF WITH PEPPERS

300 g (10 oz) lean beef steak
1 small red pepper
1 small green pepper
1 medium onion
100 g (4 oz) mushrooms
10 ml (2 tsp) olive oil
10 ml (2 tsp) tomato purée
5 ml (1 tsp) mustard
chilli sauce – to taste
125 ml (5 fl oz) water
freshly ground black pepper

Chop the onion, mushrooms and red and green peppers. Cut the steak into thin slices, about ½-inch wide by 1 inch – this is easier if the meat has been put into the freezer for about 30 minutes before being cut. Heat the oil gently in a large pan and add the onion. Cook for 10 minutes then stir in the red and green peppers and mushrooms. Cook for a further 5 minutes. Add the meat, tomato purée, mustard, chilli sauce, black pepper and water. Cook for about 8 minutes, stirring to amalgamate all the ingredients.

ORIENTAL BEEF

220 g (8 oz) lean beef steak
1 cm (½ inch) root ginger, peeled and finely chopped
4 spring onions, shredded
150 g (6 oz) beansprouts
1 small red pepper, finely chopped
15 ml (1 tbsp) olive or sunflower oil
10 ml (2 tsp) Nam Pla fish sauce
10 ml (2 tsp) soy sauce
juice of ½ orange
freshly ground black pepper

Cut the steak into slivers, ½ inch wide by 1 inch, as thinly as possible – this is easier if the meat is put into the freezer for about 30 minutes before cutting. Heat the oil in a large frying pan or wok and add the beef. Cook for 3–4 minutes, turning to brown both sides. Stir in the ginger, beansprouts and red pepper. Add the fish sauce, soy sauce, orange juice and black pepper and heat through. Stir in the spring onions and serve.

7

FAT AND FIBRE FACTS

The following pages show the fat and fibre content (per 100 g) of *Walk Slim Diet* foods and of many other foods which you may want to compare.
The following symbols are used:

0 None of the nutrient is present
Tr Trace
N The nutrient is present in significant quantities but there is no reliable information on the amount
( ) Estimated value

CEREALS, BREAD, RICE AND PASTA

	Fat g	Fibre g
Bran, wheat	5.5	36.4
Cornflour	0.7	0.1
Custard powder	0.7	(0.1)
Oatmeal, quick cook, raw	9.2	7.1
Wheat flour, brown	1.8	6.4
white, breadmaking	1.4	(3.1)
white, plain	1.3	3.1
white, self-raising	1.2	(3.1)
wholemeal	2.2	9.0
Wheatgerm	9.2	15.6
Rice – brown, raw	2.8	1.9
boiled	1.1	0.8
white, easy cook, raw	3.6	0.4
boiled	1.3	0.1
Pasta – macaroni, raw	1.8	3.1
boiled	0.5	0.9
noodles, egg, raw	8.2	(2.9)

boiled	0.5	(0.6)
spaghetti, white, raw	1.8	2.9
boiled	0.7	1.2
wholemeal, raw	2.5	8.4
boiled	0.9	3.5
Bread – brown, average	2.0	(3.5)
toasted	2.1	4.5
Chapatis, made with fat	12.8	N
made without fat	1.0	N
granary	2.7	4.3
Hovis, average	2.0	3.3
toasted	2.6	(4.2)
malt	2.4	N
Naan	12.5	1.9
Papadums, fried in oil	16.9	N
Pitta, white	1.2	2.2
Rye	1.7	4.4
Vitbe, average	3.1	(3.3)
white, average	1.9	1.5
sliced	1.3	1.5
toasted	1.6	1.8
French stick	2.7	(1.5)
wholemeal, average	2.5	(5.8)
toasted	2.9	(5.9)
Rolls – brown, crusty	2.8	(3.5)
soft	3.8	(3.5)
croissants	20.3	1.6
hamburger buns	5.0	(1.5)
white, crusty	2.3	(1.5)
soft	4.2	(1.5)
wholemeal	2.9	5.9
Breakfast cereals – All-Bran	3.4	24.5
Bran Flakes	1.9	13.0
Coco Pops	1.0	0.6
Common Sense Oat Bran Flakes	4.0	10.0
Corn Flakes	0.7	0.9
Crunchy Nut Corn Flakes	4.0	0.8

Frosties	0.5	0.6
Fruit 'n' Fibre	4.7	7.0
Muesli, Swiss style	5.9	6.4
with no		
added sugar	7.8	7.6
Porridge,		
with water	1.1	0.8
with whole		
milk	5.1	0.8
Puffed Wheat	1.3	5.6
Ready Brek	7.8	7.2
Rice Krispies	0.9	0.7
Shredded Wheat	3.0	9.8
Shreddies	1.5	9.5
Special K	1.0	2.0
Sugar Puffs	0.8	3.2
Sultana Bran	1.6	10.0
Weetabix	2.7	9.7

VEGETABLES

Asparagus – raw	0.6	1.7
boiled	0.8	1.4
Aubergine – raw	0.4	2.0
fried in corn oil	31.9	2.3
Beans – Aduki, dried, raw	0.5	11.1
dried, boiled	0.2	5.5
baked, tinned in tomato sauce	0.6	3.7
blackeye, dried, raw	1.6	8.2
dried, boiled	0.7	3.5
broad, frozen, boiled	0.6	6.5
butter, tinned, drained	0.5	4.6
chick peas, dried, raw	5.4	10.7
dried, boiled	2.1	4.3
tinned, drained	2.9	4.1
green/French, raw	0.5	2.2
frozen, boiled	0.1	4.1
Mung, dried, raw	1.1	10.0
dried, boiled	0.4	3.0

red kidney, dried, raw	1.4	15.7
dried, boiled	0.5	6.7
tinned, drained	0.6	6.2
runner, raw	0.4	2.0
boiled	0.5	1.9
soya, dried, raw	18.6	15.7
dried, boiled	7.3	6.1
Tofu, soya bean, steamed	4.2	N
steamed, fried	17.7	N
Beetroot – raw	0.1	1.9
boiled	0.1	1.9
pickled, drained	0.2	1.7
Broccoli, green – raw	0.9	2.6
boiled	0.8	2.3
Brussels sprouts – raw	1.4	4.1
boiled	1.3	3.1
frozen, boiled	(1.3)	4.3
Cabbage – raw, average	0.4	2.4
Carrots – old, raw	0.3	2.4
boiled	0.4	2.5
young, raw	0.5	2.4
boiled	0.4	2.3
canned, drained	0.3	1.9
Cauliflower – raw	0.9	1.8
boiled	0.9	1.6
Celery – raw	0.2	1.1
boiled	0.3	1.2
Chicory – raw	0.6	0.9
Courgettes – raw	0.4	0.9
boiled	0.4	1.2
fried in oil	4.8	1.2
Cucumber – raw	0.1	0.6
Fennel – raw	0.2	2.4
boiled	0.2	2.3
Garlic – raw	0.6	4.1
Leeks – raw	0.5	2.2
boiled	0.7	1.7
Lentils – green and brown, dried, raw	1.9	8.9
dried, boiled	0.7	3.8

red, split, dried, raw	1.3	4.9
dried, boiled	0.4	1.9
Lettuce – raw	0.5	0.9
Mangetout – raw	0.2	2.3
boiled	0.1	2.2
stir-fried in oil	4.8	2.4
Marrow – raw	0.2	0.5
boiled	0.2	0.6
Mushrooms – raw	0.5	1.1
boiled	0.3	1.1
fried in oil	16.2	1.5
Mustard and cress – raw	0.6	1.1
Okra – raw	1.0	4.0
boiled	0.9	3.6
fried in oil	26.1	6.3
Onions – raw	0.2	1.4
boiled	0.1	0.7
Parsnips – raw	1.1	4.6
boiled	1.2	4.7
Peas – raw	1.5	4.7
boiled	1.6	4.5
frozen, boiled	0.9	5.1
tinned, drained	0.9	5.1
processed, tinned, drained	0.7	4.8
Peppers – green, raw	0.3	1.6
boiled	0.5	1.8
red, raw	0.4	1.6
boiled	0.4	1.7
Potatoes – new, raw	0.3	1.0
boiled	0.3	1.1
in skins, boiled	0.3	1.5
tinned, drained	0.1	0.8
old, raw	0.2	1.3
baked, flesh and skin	0.2	2.7
flesh only	0.1	1.4
boiled	0.1	1.2
mashed with butter	4.3	1.1
roast in oil	4.5	1.8
in lard	4.5	1.8

chips – homemade, fried in oil	6.7	2.2
retail, fried in oil	12.4	(2.2)
French fries, retail	15.5	(2.1)
Oven chips, frozen, baked	4.2	2.0
instant potato powder – made up with water	0.1	1.0
made up with whole milk	1.2	1.0
crisps	35.9	11.9
Pumpkin – raw	0.2	1.0
boiled	0.3	1.1
Radishes – red, raw	0.2	0.9
Spinach – raw	0.8	2.1
boiled	0.8	2.1
Spring greens – raw	1.0	3.4
boiled	0.7	2.6
Spring onions – raw	0.5	1.5
Swede – raw	0.3	1.9
boiled	0.1	0.7
Sweetcorn – kernels, tinned, drained	1.2	1.4
on-the-cob, boiled	1.4	1.3
Tomato purée	0.2	2.8
Tomatoes – raw	0.3	1.0
fried in oil	7.7	1.3
grilled	0.9	2.9
tinned, whole contents	0.1	0.7
Turnip – raw	0.3	2.4
boiled	0.2	1.9
Watercress – raw	1.0	1.5

FRUIT

Apples – cooking, raw, peeled	0.1	1.6
stewed with sugar	0.1	1.2
stewed without sugar	0.1	1.5
eating, average, raw	0.1	1.8
Apricots – raw	0.1	1.7
ready-to-eat, semi-dried	0.6	6.3
tinned in syrup	0.1	0.9

tinned in juice	0.1	0.9
Avocado, average	19.5	3.4
Bananas	0.3	1.1
Blackberries – raw	0.2	3.1
stewed with sugar	0.2	2.4
stewed without sugar	0.2	2.6
Blackcurrants – raw	Tr	3.6
stewed with sugar	Tr	2.8
tinned in juice	Tr	3.1
tinned in syrup	Tr	2.6
Cherries – raw	0.1	0.9
tinned in syrup	Tr	0.6
glacé	Tr	0.9
Clementines	0.1	1.2
Currants	0.4	1.9
Damsons – raw	Tr	(1.6)
stewed with sugar	0.1	(1.5)
Dates – raw	0.2	1.5
dried	0.4	3.4
Dried mixed fruit	1.6	2.2
Figs – dried	1.5	7.5
ready to eat, semi-dried	Tr	6.9
Fruit cocktail – tinned in juice	Tr	1.0
tinned in syrup	Tr	1.0
Gooseberries – cooking, raw	0.3	2.4
stewed with sugar	0.3	1.9
stewed without sugar	0.2	2.0
Grapefruit – raw	0.1	1.3
tinned in juice	Tr	0.4
tinned in syrup	Tr	0.6
Grapes, average	0.1	0.7
Guava – raw	0.5	3.7
tinned in syrup	Tr	3.0
Kiwi fruit	0.5	1.9
Lemons – whole	0.3	N
Lychees – raw	0.1	0.7
tinned in syrup	Tr	0.5
Mandarin oranges – tinned in juice	Tr	0.3
tinned in syrup	Tr	0.2

Mangoes – ripe, raw	0.2	2.6
tinned in syrup	Tr	0.7
Melon – Cantaloup	0.1	1.0
Galia	0.1	0.4
Honeydew	0.1	0.6
watermelon	0.3	0.1
Mixed peel	0.9	4.8
Nectarines	0.1	1.2
Olives – in brine	11.0	2.9
Oranges	0.1	1.7
Passion fruit	0.4	3.3
Papaya – raw	0.1	2.2
tinned in juice	Tr	0.7
Peaches – raw	0.1	1.5
tinned in juice	Tr	0.8
tinned in syrup	Tr	0.9
Pears – average, raw	0.1	2.2
tinned in juice	Tr	1.4
tinned in syrup	Tr	1.1
Pineapple – raw	0.2	1.2
tinned in juice	Tr	0.5
tinned in syrup	Tr	0.7
Plums – average, raw	0.1	1.6
stewed with sugar	0.1	1.2
stewed without sugar	0.1	1.2
tinned in syrup	Tr	0.8
Prunes – tinned in juice	0.2	2.4
tinned in syrup	0.2	2.8
ready-to-eat, semi-dried	0.4	5.7
Raisins	0.4	2.0
Raspberries – raw	0.3	2.5
tinned in syrup	0.1	1.5
Rhubarb – raw	0.1	1.4
stewed with sugar	0.1	1.2
stewed without sugar	0.1	1.3
tinned in syrup	Tr	0.8
Satsumas	0.1	1.3
Strawberries – raw	0.1	1.2
tinned in syrup	Tr	0.7

Sultanas	0.4	2.0
Tangerines	0.1	1.3

White Fish

Cod – raw, fillets	0.7	0
baked, fillets	1.2	0
poached, fillets	1.1	0
frozen, raw, steaks	0.6	0
grilled, steaks	1.3	0
in batter, fried in oil	10.3	(0.3)
Haddock – raw	0.6	0
steamed	0.8	0
in crumbs, fried in oil	8.3	(0.2)
smoked, steamed	0.9	0
Halibut – raw	2.4	0
steamed	4.0	0
Lemon Sole – raw	1.4	0
steamed	0.9	0
in crumbs, fried	13.0	(0.4)
Plaice – raw	2.2	0
steamed	1.9	0
in batter, fried in oil	18.0	N
in crumbs, fried, fillets	13.7	N
Skate – in batter, fried	12.1	(0.2)
Whiting – steamed	0.9	0
in crumbs, fried	10.3	(0.3)

Fatty Fish

Anchovies – tinned in oil, drained	19.9	0
Herring – raw	18.5	0
fried	15.1	N
grilled	13.0	0
Kipper – baked	11.4	0
Mackerel – raw	16.3	0

fried	11.3	0
smoked	30.9	0
Pilchards, tinned in tomato sauce	5.4	Tr
Salmon – raw	(12.0)	0
steamed	13.0	0
tinned	8.2	0
smoked	4.5	0
Sardines – tinned in tomato sauce	11.6	Tr
tinned in oil, drained	13.6	0
Trout – brown, steamed	4.5	0
Tuna – tinned in oil, drained	9.0	0
tinned in brine, drained	0.6	0
Whitebait – fried	47.5	0.2

Other Seafood

Crab – boiled	5.2	0
boiled, weighed with shell	1.0	0
tinned	0.9	0
Lobster – boiled	3.4	0
boiled, weighed with shell	1.2	0
Prawns – boiled	1.8	0
boiled, weighed with shell	0.7	0
Scampi – in breadcrumbs, frozen, fried	17.6	N
Shrimps – frozen, shell removed	0.8	0
tinned, drained	1.2	0
Cockles – boiled	0.3	0
Mussels – boiled	2.0	0
boiled, weighed with shell	0.6	0
Oysters – raw	0.9	0
Scallops – steamed	1.4	0
Squid – frozen, raw	1.5	0
Swordfish – raw	4.0	0
Whelks – boiled, weighed with shell	0.3	0
Winkles – boiled, weighed with shell	0.3	0

Fish Products

Fish cakes – fried	10.5	N
Fish fingers – fried, in oil	12.7	0.6
grilled	9.0	0.7
Fish paste	10.4	(0.2)
Fish pie	3.0	0.7
Kedgeree	7.9	Tr
Taramasalata	46.4	N

Poultry and Game

Chicken – meat only, raw	4.3	0
meat and skin, raw	17.7	0
light meat, raw	3.2	0
dark meat, raw	5.5	0
boiled, meat only	7.3	0
light meat	4.9	0
dark meat	9.9	0
roast, meat only	5.4	0
meat and skin	14.0	0
light meat	4.0	0
dark meat	6.9	0
wing quarter, roast, meat only		
weighed with bone	2.7	0
leg quarter, roast, meat only		
weighed with bone	3.4	0
breaded, fried in vegetable oil	12.7	0.7
Duck – meat only, raw	4.8	0
meat, fat and skin, raw	42.7	0
roast, meat only	9.7	0
meat, fat and skin	29.0	0
Goose – roast, meat only	22.4	0
Grouse – roast, meat only	5.3	0
roast, weighed with bone	3.5	0
Partridge – roast, meat only	7.2	0

roast, weighed with bone	4.3	0
Pheasant – roast, meat only	9.3	0
roast, weighed with bone	5.9	0
Pigeon – roast, meat only	13.2	0
roast, weighed with bone	5.8	0
Turkey – meat only, raw	2.2	0
meat and skin, raw	6.9	0
light meat, raw	1.1	0
dark meat, raw	3.6	0
roast, meat only	2.7	0
meat and skin	6.5	0
light meat	1.4	0
dark meat	4.1	0
Rabbit – meat only, raw	4.0	0
stewed, meat only	7.7	0
weighed with bone	3.9	0
Venison – roast	6.4	0

Other Meats

Bacon – gammon rasher, lean and fat, grilled	12.2	0
lean only, grilled	5.2	0
rasher, lean and fat, raw	41.2	0
lean only, fried	22.3	0
lean and fat, fried	40.6	0
lean only, grilled	18.9	0
lean and fat, grilled	33.8	0
ham – tinned	5.1	0
Beef – forerib, lean and fat, raw	25.1	0
roast	28.8	0
lean only, roast	12.6	0
mince, raw	16.2	0
stewed	15.2	0
rump steak, lean and fat, raw	13.5	0
fried	14.6	0
grilled	12.1	0
lean only, fried	7.4	0

grilled	6.0	0
sirloin – lean and fat, raw	22.8	0
roast	21.1	0
lean only, roast	9.1	0
stewing steak – lean and fat, raw	10.6	0
stewed	11.0	0
topside, lean and fat, raw	11.2	0
roast	12.0	0
lean only, roast	4.4	0
Lamb – chops, loin, lean and fat, raw	35.4	0
grilled	29.0	0
loin, lean only, grilled	12.3	0
cutlets, lean and fat, raw	36.3	0
grilled	30.9	0
lean only, grilled	12.3	0
leg, lean and fat, raw	18.7	0
roast	17.9	0
lean only, roast	8.1	0
Pork – chops, loin, lean and fat, raw	29.5	0
grilled	24.2	0
loin, lean only, grilled	10.7	0
leg, lean and fat, raw	22.5	0
roast	19.8	0
lean only, roast	6.9	0
Veal – cutlet, fried in oil	8.1	(0.1)
fillet, raw	2.7	0
roast	11.5	0

Offal

Heart – lamb, raw	5.6	0
sheep, roast	14.7	0
Kidney – lamb, raw	2.7	0
fried	6.3	0
pig, raw	2.7	0
stewed	6.1	0
Liver – calf, raw	7.3	0
fried	13.2	0.2

chicken, raw	6.3	0
fried	10.9	0.2
lamb, raw	10.3	0
fried	14.0	0.1
Oxtail, stewed	13.4	0
Sweetbread, lamb, raw	7.8	0
fried	14.6	(0.1)
Tongue, lamb, raw	14.6	0
sheep, stewed	24.0	0
Tripe, dressed	2.5	0
dressed, stewed	4.5	0

Meat Products

Beefburgers, frozen, raw	20.5	N
frozen, fried	17.3	N
Black pudding, fried	21.9	N
Corned beef, tinned	12.1	0
Cornish pastie	20.4	0.9
Frankfurters	25.0	0.1
Grillsteaks, grilled	23.9	Tr
Haggis, boiled	21.7	N
Ham and pork, chopped, tinned	23.6	0.3
Liver sausage	26.9	0.5
Luncheon meat, tinned	26.9	0.3
Meat paste	11.2	0.1
Pâté, liver	28.9	Tr
low fat	12.0	Tr
Pork pie, individual	27.0	0.9
Salami	45.2	0.1
Sausage roll, flaky pastry	36.4	1.2
short pastry	31.9	1.4
Sausages – beef, raw	24.1	0.5
fried	18.0	0.7
grilled	17.3	0.7
pork, raw	32.1	0.5
fried	24.5	0.7
grilled	24.6	0.7

low fat, raw	9.5	1.2
fried	13.0	1.4
grilled	13.8	1.5
Saveloy	20.5	N
Steak and kidney pie, individual	21.2	0.9
pastry top only	18.4	0.6
Stewed steak, tinned, with gravy	12.5	Tr
Tongue, tinned	16.5	0

EGGS

Eggs – chicken, whole, raw	10.8	0
white, raw	Tr	0
yolk, raw	30.5	0
boiled	10.8	0
fried in oil	13.9	0
poached	10.8	0
scrambled, with milk	22.6	0

Egg Dishes

Meringue	Tr	0
with cream	23.6	0
omelette, plain	16.4	0
quiche, cheese and egg	22.2	0.6
Scotch eggs, retail	17.1	N

NUTS AND SEEDS

Almonds	55.8	(7.4)
weighed with shells	20.6	(2.7)
Brazil nuts	68.2	4.3
weighed with shells	31.4	2.0
Cashew nuts, roasted and salted	50.9	3.2
Chestnuts	2.7	4.1
Coconut – creamed block	68.8	N
desiccated	62.0	13.7
Hazelnuts	63.5	6.5
weighed with shells	24.1	2.5

Macadamia nuts, salted	77.6	5.3
Marzipan, homemade	25.8	(3.3)
retail	14.4	(1.9)
Peanut butter, smooth	53.7	5.4
Peanuts – plain	46.1	6.2
plain, weighed with shells	31.8	4.3
dry roasted	49.8	6.4
roasted and salted	53.0	6.0
Pecan nuts	70.1	4.7
Pine nuts	68.6	1.9
Pistachio nuts, weighed with shells	30.5	3.3
Sesame seeds	58.0	7.9
Sunflower seeds	47.5	6.0
Tahini paste	58.9	8.0
Walnuts	68.5	3.5
weighed with shells	29.4	1.5

MILK AND DAIRY FOODS

skimmed milk, average	0.1	0
semi-skimmed milk, average	1.6	0
whole milk, average	3.9	0
condensed milk, skimmed, sweetened	0.2	0
whole, sweetened	10.1	0
dried skimmed milk	0.6	0
with vegetable fat	25.9	0
evaporated milk, whole	9.4	0
fresh creams (pasteurised) – half	13.3	0
single	19.1	0
soured	19.9	0
whipping	39.3	0
double	48.0	0
clotted	63.5	0
Cheese – Brie	26.9	0
Camembert	23.7	0
Cheddar, average	34.4	0
vegetarian	35.7	0
reduced fat	15.0	0
cheese spread, plain	22.8	0

cottage cheese, plain	3.9	0
reduced fat	1.4	0
cream cheese	47.4	0
Danish Blue	29.6	0
Edam	25.4	0
Feta	20.2	0
fromage frais, fruit	5.8	Tr
plain	7.1	0
very low fat	0.2	Tr
full fat soft cheese	31.0	0
Gouda	31.0	0
Gorgonzola	28.4	0
Gruyère	33.3	0
hard cheese, average	34.0	0
medium fat soft cheese	14.5	0
Parmesan	32.7	0
processed cheese, plain	27.0	0
Roquefort	32.9	0
Stilton, blue	35.5	0
white cheese, average	31.3	0
yogurt – Greek, cows	9.1	0
sheep	7.5	0
low calorie	0.2	N
low fat, plain	0.8	N
flavoured	0.9	N
fruit	0.7	N
tzatziki	4.9	0.2
whole milk, plain	3.0	N
fruit	2.8	N
Arctic roll	6.6	Tr
Choc ice	17.5	Tr
Chocolate nut sundae	15.3	0.1
Cornetto	12.9	N
frozen ice cream desserts	14.2	Tr
ice cream – dairy, vanilla	9.8	Tr
flavoured	8.0	Tr
non-dairy, vanilla	8.7	Tr
flavoured	7.4	Tr
sorbet, lemon	Tr	0

cheesecake, frozen	10.6	(0.9)
crème caramel	2.2	N
custard, made with whole milk	4.5	Tr
made with skimmed milk	0.1	Tr
tinned	3.0	(0.1)
instant dessert powder	17.3	(1.0)
made with whole milk	6.3	(0.2)
made with skimmed milk	3.2	(0.2)
milk pudding,		
made with whole milk	4.3	0.1
made with skimmed milk	0.2	0.1
mousse, chocolate	5.4	N
fruit	5.7	N
rice pudding, tinned	2.5	0.2

FATS AND OILS

Spreading Fats

Butter	81.7	0
Dairy/fat spread	73.4	0
Low fat spread	40.5	0
Margarine	81.6	0
very low fat spread	25.0	0

Animal Fats

dripping, beef	99.0	0
lard	99.0	0
suet, shredded	86.7	0.5

Oils

coconut oil	99.9	0
cod liver oil	99.9	0
corn	99.9	0

olive	99.9	0
safflower oil	99.9	0
sunflower seed oil	99.9	0
vegetable oil, blended, average	99.9	0

SOUPS AND SAUCES

Tinned Soups

cream of chicken, ready to serve	3.8	N
condensed	7.2	N
ready to serve	3.6	N
cream of mushroom, ready to serve	3.8	N
cream of tomato, ready to serve	3.3	N
condensed	6.8	N
ready to serve	3.4	N
low calorie, tomato, vegetable and mine-		
strone	0.2	N
oxtail, ready to serve	1.7	N
vegetable, ready to serve	0.7	1.5

Packet Soups

chicken noodle, dried	5.0	4.3
ready to serve	0.3	0.2
Minestrone, dried	8.8	N
ready to serve	0.7	N
oxtail, dried	10.5	N
ready to serve	0.8	N
tomato, dried	5.6	N
ready to serve	0.5	N

Dairy Sauces

bread sauce, made with whole milk	5.1	0.3
made with semi-skimmed milk	3.1	0.3
cheese sauce, made with whole milk	14.6	0.2
made with semi-skimmed milk	12.6	0.2

cheese sauce packet mix,		
made with whole milk	6.1	N
made with semi-skimmed milk	3.8	N
onion sauce,		
made with whole milk	6.5	0.4
made with semi-skimmed milk	5.0	0.4
white sauce, savoury,		
made with whole milk	10.3	0.2
made with semi-skimmed milk	7.8	0.2
sweet, made with whole milk	9.5	0.2
made with semi-skimmed milk	7.2	0.2

Salad Sauces, Dressings and Pickles

apple chutney	0.2	1.2
French dressing	72.1	0
mango chutney	10.9	0.9
mayonnaise, retail	75.6	0
pickle, sweet	0.3	1.2
salad cream	31.0	N
reduced calorie	17.2	N
tomato chutney	0.4	1.4

Non-salad Sauces

barbecue sauce	1.8	N
brown sauce, bottled	0	0.7
cook-in-sauces, tinned	0.8	N
curry sauce, tinned	5.0	N
horseradish sauce	8.4	2.5
mint sauce	Tr	N
pasta sauce, tomato based	1.5	N
soy sauce	0	0
tomato ketchup	Tr	0.9
tomato sauce	5.5	1.4

Sugars, Syrups and Preserves

chocolate nut spread	33.0	0.8
honey	0	0
honeycomb	4.6	0
jam, fruit with edible seeds	0	N
reduced sugar	0.1	N
lemon curd	5.1	(0.2)
marmalade	0	(0.6)
mincemeat	4.3	1.3
sugar, demerara	0	0
white	0	0
syrup, golden	0	0
treacle, black	0	0

Chocolate Confectionery

Bounty bar	26.1	N
chocolate, milk	30.3	Tr
plain	29.2	N
white	30.9	0
chocolates, fancy and filled	18.8	N
creme eggs	16.8	Tr
Kit Kat	26.6	N
Mars bar	18.9	Tr
Milky Way	15.8	Tr
Twix	24.5	N

Non-chocolate Confectionery

boiled sweets	Tr	0
fruit gums	0	0
liquorice allsorts	2.2	N
pastilles	0	0
peppermints	0.7	0
popcorn, candied	20.0	N

plain	42.8	N
toffees, mixed	17.2	0
Turkish delight, without nuts	0	0

Savoury Snacks

Bombay mix	32.9	6.2
corn snacks	31.9	1.0
peanuts and raisins	26.0	4.4
potato crisps	37.6	4.9
low fat	21.5	6.3
potato hoops	32.0	2.6
Tortilla chips	22.6	4.9
Twiglets	11.7	10.3

CAKES, BISCUITS, PASTRIES AND SAVOURIES

biscuits – chocolate, full-coated	27.6	2.1
cream crackers	16.3	2.2
crispbread, rye	2.1	11.7
digestive, chocolate	24.1	2.2
plain	20.9	2.2
flapjacks	26.6	2.7
gingernut	15.2	1.4
Jaffa cakes	10.5	N
shortbread	26.1	1.9
wafer, filled	29.9	N
wholemeal crackers	11.3	4.4
cakes – Battenburg	17.5	N
fruit, plain, retail	12.9	N
rich	11.0	1.7
rich, iced	11.4	1.7
Madeira	16.9	0.9
sponge, basic recipe	26.3	0.9
fatless	6.1	0.9
jam filled	4.9	1.8
with butter icing	30.6	0.6
Swiss rolls, chocolate, individual	11.3	N

pastry – flaky, raw	30.7	1.4
cooked	40.6	1.8
shortcrust, raw	27.9	1.9
cooked	32.3	2.2
wholemeal, raw	28.4	5.4
cooked	32.9	6.3
buns and pastries – crumpets, toasted	1.0	(2.0)
currant buns	7.5	N
custard tarts	14.5	1.2
Danish pastries	17.6	1.6
doughnuts, jam	14.5	N
ring	21.7	N
eclairs, frozen	30.6	0.8
hot cross buns	6.8	1.7
jam tarts	14.9	1.6
mince pies	20.4	2.1
scones, fruit	9.8	N
plain	14.6	1.9
wholemeal	14.4	5.2
Scotch pancakes	11.7	1.4
teacakes, toasted	8.3	N
puddings – bread	9.6	1.2
Christmas	9.7	1.3
crumble, fruit	6.9	1.7
fruit pie, one crust	7.9	1.7
pastry top and bottom	13.3	1.8
wholemeal, one crust	8.1	2.7
pastry top and bottom	13.6	3.5
lemon meringue pie	14.4	0.7
pancakes, sweet, made with		
whole milk	16.2	0.8
sponge	16.3	1.1
treacle tart	14.1	1.1
savouries – cauliflower cheese	6.9	1.3
dumplings	11.7	0.9
macaroni cheese	10.8	0.5
pancakes, savoury, made with		
whole milk	17.5	0.8
pizza	11.8	1.5

frozen	10.7	(1.5)
ravioli, tinned in tomato sauce	2.2	0.9
samosas, meat	56.1	1.2
vegetable	41.8	1.8
spaghetti, tinned in tomato sauce	0.4	0.7
stuffing, sage and onion	14.8	1.7
stuffing mix	5.2	4.7
made with water	1.5	1.3
Yorkshire pudding	9.9	0.9

MISCELLANEOUS FOODS

baking powder	Tr	0
Bovril	0.7	0
gelatin	0	0
gravy instant granules	32.5	Tr
made with water	2.4	Tr
Marmite	0.7	0
mustard, smooth	8.2	N
wholegrain	10.2	4.9
Oxo cubes	3.4	0
salt, block	0	0
table	0	0
vinegar	0	0
water	0	0
yeast, bakers, compressed	0.4	N
dried	1.5	N

DRINKS

Powdered Drinks and Essences

Bournvita powder	1.5	N
made with whole milk	3.8	Tr
made with semi-skimmed milk	1.6	Tr
cocoa powder	21.7	12.1
made with whole milk	4.2	0.2

made with semi-skimmed milk	1.9	0.2
coffee, instant	0	0
Coffeemate	34.9	0
Drinking chocolate powder	6.0	N
made with whole milk	4.1	Tr
made with semi-skimmed milk	1.9	Tr
Horlicks Lowfat Instant powder	3.3	N
made with water	0.5	Tr
Horlicks powder	4.0	N
made with whole milk	3.9	Tr
made with semi-skimmed milk	1.9	Tr
milk shake powder	1.6	Tr
made with whole milk	3.7	Tr
made with semi-skimmed milk	1.6	Tr
Ovaltine powder	2.7	N
made with whole milk	3.8	Tr
made with semi-skimmed milk	1.7	Tr
Tea, Indian	Tr	0

Carbonated Drinks

Coca-cola	0	0
lemonade, bottled	0	0
Lucozade	0	0

Squash and Cordials

lime juice cordial, undiluted	0	0
orange juice, undiluted	0	0
Ribena, undiluted	0	0
rosehip syrup, undiluted	0	0

Juices

apple juice, unsweetened	0.1	Tr
grape juice, unsweetened	0.1	0
grapefruit juice, unsweetened	0.1	Tr
lemon juice	Tr	0.1

orange juice, unsweetened	0.1	0.1
pineapple juice, unsweetened	0.1	Tr
tomato juice	Tr	0.6

ALCOHOLIC DRINKS (PER 100 ML)

Beers

beer, bitter, canned	Tr	0
draught	Tr	0
keg	Tr	0
mild, draught	Tr	0
brown ale, bottled	Tr	0
lager, bottled	Tr	0
pale ale, bottled	Tr	0
stout, bottled	Tr	0
strong ale	Tr	0

Ciders

cider, dry	0	0
sweet	0	0
vintage	0	0

Wines

red wine	0	0
rosé wine, medium	0	0
white wine, dry	0	0
medium	0	0
sparkling	0	0
sweet	0	0

Fortified Wines

Port	0	0
Sherry, dry	0	0
medium	0	0
sweet	0	0

Vermouths

Vermouth, dry	0	0
sweet	0	0

Spirits

40% volume	0	0

THE WALK SLIM VIDEO

If you would like to follow the 30 Day Walkout and the Whole-Body Workout on video then WALK SLIM is available at £12.99 from all main video outlets.

THE WALK SLIM AUDIO TAPE

If you would like to listen while you walk, the WALK SLIM 60-minute instructional audio tape will keep you motivated and take you through the 30 Day Walkout. Available at £9.99 from KSSK Music Ltd, 37 Pandora Road, West Hampstead, London NW6 1TS. Tel: 071 431 3114.